HEAD IN THE CLOUDS

MEMORIES AND REFLECTIONS

Boyd Clack is an actor, writer and singer-songwriter from Wales. Best known in Wales as creator, writer, leading actor in long running BAFTA winning and nominated TV Sit Com's *Satellite City* and *High Hopes*, he trained at The Royal Welsh College of Music and Drama receiving Best Actor award. His many acting credits on stage include one man plays *Underground Man* (Edinburgh Festival), *Fallen Angel* (The Bush), Sir William Rhys in Robert Lepage's magnificent *Tectonic Plates* at The National Theatres of England and Canada, *Midsummer's Night Dream* (Moving Being), *Macbeth* at Leicester Haymarket, *Hamlet* at The Young Vic, Steven Berkoff's *Coriolanus* at The West Yorkshire Playhouse. He spoke the first words on stage for The National Theatre of Wales' inaugural production *A Good Night Out in the Valleys* playing Con to huge critical acclaim. He recently made a debut in musicals as Frank in *Half 'n' Half* at Wales Millennium Centre to great reviews: 'a masterclass in comedic timing, underpinned by a depth and pathos which shouts out for a big serious role for one of Wales's underused great dramatic talents.' *The Western Mail.*

Television credits include leading roles as Dezmond Rezzilo in two series of *The Celluloid World of Dezmond Rezzilo*, Gwynne Price in three series of *Satellite City* and Sgt Arthur Ball in six series and three specials of *High Hopes*. Other notable roles in drama series include *House of Cards*, *A Small Summer Party*, *New Tricks*, *Being Human*, *Baker Boys*, *The Green Hollow* and *Keeping Faith*.

His film credits include *Tectonic Plates*, *Twin Town*, *The Testament of Taliesin Jones* and *Risen*, for which he received International Film Awards for Best Supporting Actor (2010) and Action On Film Nominee (California) (2011) for his portrayal of Howard Winstone Senior. He played Mr Pugh in Kevin Allen's Oscar nominated *Under Milk Wood* and will soon be seen in *Eternal Beauty* (2019).

Boyd Clack has also released albums of his own compositions – *Welsh Bitter* and *Labourer of Love*. A supporter of a number of charities Boyd is Patron of New Horizons Mental Health Charity; Joint Patron with his partner, co-writer of *High Hopes*, actress and producer Kirsten Jones, for Royal Commonwealth Society (Wales), Cardiff Mini Film Festival; Greyhound Rescue Wales.

Boyd continues to act and write and says he will do so until the shutters come down and the shop is closed.

Head in the Clouds

Memories and Reflections

Boyd Clack

Parthian, Cardigan SA43 1ED
www.parthianbooks.com
First published in 2018
© Boyd Clack 2018
ISBN 978-1-912681-01-3
Edited by Edward Matthews
Creative Consultant Kirsten Jones
Cover Photography by Kirsten Jones
Cover Design by Marc Jennings
Typeset by Alison Evans
Printed by Pulsio

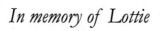

In memory of Lottie

CONTENTS

CHILDHOOD

#1

I used to imagine, half dream, that I was me as a little boy lying in bed in Stalag 2, my bedroom as a child, and I would wake, walk over to the window and our back garden would be lit up in a light blue, almost violet, light and there would be white marble statues on the lawn – classical statues of muscular yet contemplative men and beautiful women from antiquity. I would look over at the silhouetted roofs of Pretoria Road beyond and find myself flying, or floating, above them, closer to the blackness of the sky. Next I would suddenly find myself walking along the pathway that led beside the Battlefield near the farm that overlooked our house. It was a walk I often went on summer evenings with my old man ... across the Waun to Coedely colliery in the twilight, the church bells calling the old men and women to church. Finally it would be later, the middle of the night, and I would be on a beach in the moonlight staring out at the huge ocean before me. I would feel in awe of the universe, the lapping of the waves the only noise disturbing the infinite silence. I'd be in my stripy pyjamas, the uniform of God's little soldiers. I have lived this scenario many hundreds of times. I'd go to bed when it was still light and read my popup books while eating bread and butter and jam and buttered Marie biscuits and drinking a glass of milk. This was the Last Supper. As a child my mind was awash with religious imagery. I'd sit on the Gas House roof by the old chapel with my friend Gwynne and feel God's presence in the warm air. I was always ready to be lifted up by his unseen hand, to be held up in the sky with a billion eyes gazing down on me. The negative aspect was when it became entangled with my fears. I once saw the Virgin Mary standing on the landing. She was shrouded in a green glow, reading from a big book. I was lifted by dream beings and pulled

1

along towards her but I felt terrified and screamed out. Why would I feel terrified of Jesus's mother? Because I was terrified of death! Not the physical reality of death but the doorway to unspeakable strangeness that it opened. I was utterly alone you see. I had no control over anything. I still feel the ghostly image of that helplessness sometimes. I never feel safe. We children are just characters in dark fairy tales. We have to do what the story says.

My father died when I was three years old. He'd been seriously ill since I was born, in and out of hospital and was being treated for leukaemia then he died. We were living in a white wooden house in Courtney, Vancouver where I was born. My father had been a prisoner of war of the Germans and his illness was attributable to his mistreatment there. My childhood to that point was dominated by a mood of expectant death, a mood that informed every moment. The house was a house of death. After he died my mother brought me, my brother and sister, back to Wales and I ended up being 'adopted' by my uncle and aunt in Tonyrefail. We lived in the Avenue and I had a small, long, narrow room with a window onto the street and an attic door. This was my first bedroom, which I called Stalag 1 after my father's prison camp. It became a hall of horror to me. My mind was awash with the perfume of death. I was terrified of the dark. It heralded the arrival of a parade of monstrous hallucinations. It was a pantomime of death, monsters, ghosts, dead people, werewolves, cowled monks, creatures from the depths of the Id. The room itself was a coffin, my coffin. Jesus watched on, the Virgin read from her ancient book but no-one helped. A child's relationship to huge concepts, such as death, is not intellectual. It is a thing of images and intangible fears. My childhood horror, the presence of the watching figure of death, has never left me. I can hardly breathe with it sometimes. I wish I could be freed from it but I fear it has become a part of me to such an extent that I couldn't function without it. If you have children, don't dismiss what may appear to you to be their foolish or whimsical fears. Try to understand them from the little one's point of view. Comfort them. Give them love and protection from the darkness. Love to you all my fellow darklings.

THE CHILDREN OF THE DAMNED

When me, my brother and sister were children
After my father had died
They lived with our mother
Down by the seaside.
I lived with my uncle and auntie
In their valleys home,
They fed me and protected me
As if I was their own.
But us kids, we missed each other.
We'd been a little band
Me, my brother and sister
The Children of the Damned.

When I was at infants' school
They told me Jesus was meek and mild
But my mother was violent
And my brother and sister ran wild.
I slept on my own in a coffin.
While they slept in a burning room
We wanted to be together
By the light of the silvery moon.
We reached out for each other.
We were fingers on one hand.
Me, my brother and sister
The Children of the Damned.

#4

All men and quite a few women will be aware that when semen comes into contact with water, in the bath for example, it acquires a colourless rubbery form. When I was a sex-obsessed teenager this was not an uncommon scenario so I decided rather than just let it go down the plug with the water, I'd save it. Then came the question of what to do with it (it being essentially uninteresting in its un-sculpted form) so I decided to make little men from it, models of soldiers in fact. It took a lot of time and effort, the shields and spears were particularly tricky, but after three years or so I had a small army of these Sperm Men. I even had several battle horses and an ancient catapult. They were lined along the edge of the mantelpiece, on top of the wardrobe and on the dressing table up in my bedroom, eternally vigilant, waiting for their moment to come, so to speak. A battle was brewing in the hidden world of fairies and dream warriors and my Sperm Men were ready to play their part. I'd lie in bed at night and see them gathered there, ghostly, glowing in the gentle reflected moonlight that fell on them through the flimsy curtains. It was as if they were luminous, a vast army of godly crusaders. They never moved. They were made of heavenly Jade. My mother gave them away to a jumble sale when I was in college and I never saw them again. I was angry but maybe they'd served their purpose for me. I hope they found a good owner, someone who saw that were created from the very essence of life, out of raw love. If you have them give them my regards and say 'Chins up. The battle is yet to come little ones. The universe is still evolving'…

… The little ones spurned dancing or any other artistic pursuit. They were born to fight. I failed to make it clear how close we became. I loved them and they respected me. I think

5

they regarded me as a planet.

There were no sperm women unfortunately so their existence is finite unless Ova Women exist. I have a female friend who used to make jewellery from sperm, rings, bracelets and necklaces. She was lovely. Love to you all.

I lived with my auntie and uncle when I was a boy, but spent the holidays with my mother, brother and sister in Pontycymmer. I got to know a few friends there, one of which was a young girl and her brother. They were the same age as me, seven or eightish. The girl's name was Sonia and we struck up a close friendship. She was lovely and very pretty, but she was ill. I didn't understand what the illness was but one day they told me she had died. I was very upset, but more because she was gone than that she was actually dead. I didn't understand what it meant. A year later I was back in Pontycymmer and went over to call on her brother to go out and play. When I got there he was getting dressed upstairs, so I stood in the kitchen waiting for him. It was one of those small rooms at the back of the house. It was latish afternoon on a cold but clear day; the blue sky was fading outside, wisps of cloud dissolving into nothingness. The room itself was unlit and being overlooked by the side of the house next door, gloomy and silent. The fire was dying in the grate and my friend's father was sat alone at the table eating his tea. It was pilchards in tomato sauce. We didn't speak or make eye contact, just there together with the sound of his knife and fork scraping the plate. It was eerie and sad. Then he suddenly dropped the cutlery onto the plate and let out a fearful moan. He was a big man, a miner, tough looking and it was unreal to see him burst into tears, not just crying but sobbing, wailing in agony. I stood not knowing what to do. The food dribbled from his mouth as he rent the heavens. What unhappiness was there, what unspeakable pain; his little girl had been taken from him. He was heartbroken in a way that hearts can never be mended. I thought of this recently when sunlight fell into a room in my house in the same way: dull and mocking. Life truly is a veil of tears.

7

MOTHER RITTER

Mother Ritter, old and bitter
Murdered children in the winter,
Threw their bodies down a well
Goodbye Johnny, Liz and Nel.

Mother Ritter, constant knitter
Killed her neighbour's baby sister,
Little Lily sweet and pretty
Axed to pieces with no pity.

Mother Ritter killed the vicar
Stuck a pitchfork in his ticker
When he found the murdered children
And figured out who must have killed'em

Mother Ritter, Mother Ritter
Was a scratcher and a spitter
Bit her sister's finger off
As they dragged her from the loft.

Mother Ritter, Evil critter,
Throat of new born baby slitter
Left to rot in a stinking shed
God damn her soul: Thank God she's dead.
God damn her soul. Thank God she's DEAD!

At Christmas each year, my mind strays to my childhood. A big fire, a tree, fairy lights, trimmings, baubles, presents wrapped in Christmas paper. We'd have a big fry up for breakfast and the difficulties of life would be forgotten for the day. The falling snow would wash the world white and the moon and starlight would sprinkle it with a timeless magic. I had a fort with soldiers one year including a box of soldiers from my sister-in-law Frances's brother Billie. I had a red three-wheel tricycle from which my mother stole the boot to use as a bread bin on another. These along with the chemistry sets and compendia of games and the quiz where a little plastic robot man would rotate and point to the right answers remain firmly rooted in my memory. Life was so much simpler then. My eyes are damp with tears for all the loved ones I have lost since then. My religion is pure and unsullied. I use the language of Christianity because I was brought up in the church and I still love Jesus and his teachings. I would ask those who decry Christianity to remember that that is a vile corruption of the true message which remains a beacon of goodness in a dark world. Peace and love to you all.

DAISY DAISY

Daisy danced
In the polka dot lights
Medicated
And free
Oh Auntie Daisy
Remember me?
Will's little boy
Barbara's little friend!
I have grown
The Crown of Thorns
Or the diamond face
Barbara
No questions
Between us ever
No channelling
Of directionless hate
I am cut up
That you were taken away
To the world of the mad
And I didn't even
Acknowledge it
This enormous thing
That had happened
To my childhood friend
My dear childhood friend
And her fragile
Tragic mother.

I was living in Jersey in the summer of 1970. I was nineteen.
I was a recently formed hippie and I would walk around in St
Hellier or Goree near the mental hospital where I was working
in red velvet trousers, a shirt with lines of tiny roses and shoes
with an American flag design. It was a beautiful summer that
year. I'd wander down Daisy Hill to the Dolphin pub on the
harbour hand-in-hand with the delectable Pauline who wore
white socks and have a few beers and listen to Barney the
Irishman singing rebel songs to the tourists. I didn't really know
anyone, no-one cared about me, I had no measurable talent or
anything that others would consider special about me. I was just
a thin bespectacled youth, a sort of walking dandelion, and yet
I felt special. I felt that I was magical and delicate, a child of
the sun. I mean, don't get me wrong, I'd be sad, I'd cry, I'd get
drunk, I'd sit on the beach at Arichondel Bay and stare out into
the ocean in the nights, watch the tiny lights of the cars on the
coast of France and be overwhelmed with surges of emotion,
of love and fear and wonder. I have never felt as alive as I did
then. The resonance of that time has faded slowly but steadily
throughout the passing years. This is why things from that time,
the late sixties, have affected the rest of my life so profoundly.
That is why the music of the time, films, literature, television,
news stories – The Beatles, Haight Ashbury, fashion, all of it
means so much to me. It invokes memory of that feeling, an
innocent self-awareness. I had known love by then, romantic,
intense love and I was actually in love with every girl I saw, every
one of them, just passing in the street or near me in a café.
I was in love with them and they were in love with me. Our
eyes would meet for possibly the only time in our lives, and for
just that moment we would both know we were in love. I felt

as though I was a part of everything. Time was still. It would never go forward, never go back, there was just the moment. I've never experienced this since. Everything seems in transition since then, always a step towards something else. I was in some sort of divine state I suppose. Yes ... the perfect innocence of childhood was what it was. Nothing compares.

I worked for a time as a student nurse in a large old Victorian mental asylum in Bridgend. I lived in. My room was actually on a ward, a side room. There was a patient named Mister Arnold who had his own room, a side room off one of the corridors. He was about fifty and had a receding hairline and an aquiline, birdlike face. His family were well-to-do. He'd been a barrister or some such thing. He was always immaculately dressed ... expensive three-piece suits ... tweed ... Harris tweed ... My mother would have been very impressed ... yes ... he didn't socialise, not at all. I mean he'd reply politely if you asked him a question or return a greeting, a good morning ... but he'd never instigate conversation. I was passing his room one evening ... it was night time in fact ... and his door happened to be ajar ... I noticed him ... he was moving around ... so I stopped and observed him unseen. He went to a chest of drawers, opened the bottom one and took out a folded sheet ... a white bed sheet ... then he went over to a dressing table ... old fashioned, you know with a mirror, and he threw the sheet over it so it was covered ... like a dust sheet over something in storage ... then he adjusted it with infinite patience till it was as he wanted it and then he gazed at it for a few moments satisfying himself that it was ... perfect. Finally he stepped away over to the far side of the room and shielding his face from the spectre he had just so carefully and lovingly created he fell to his knees screaming ... really terrible screams ... blood curdling screams ... from the depths of his being ... he was crying too ... crying and screaming out 'No! No! Keep away from me! Leave me in peace! Aaaaah! Aaaaah! Please God Protect me! Aaaah!' And ... it carried on unwavering in its intensity for minutes and then ... he stopped ... just like that and there was silence. He stood up, walked over to the dressing table, removed the sheet, refolded it carefully as it had been before, returned it to the open drawer and shut it away again. And you know ... he sat on the side of the bed and ... took out a cigarette ... an untipped cigarette ... lit it with his gold lighter and sat there calm and ... blew thick clouds of smoke into the air above him and ... I have never seen a man look more relaxed ... more at peace. Yes ... yes indeed.

#11

When I was fifteen I got a job in the school holiday packing shelves in what we would now call a supermarket. I was immature for my age, never had a girlfriend, never been kissed though, as boys of that age invariably do, I had begun thinking of girls lustfully on an almost permanent basis. The girls working there delighted in embarrassing me. It would make them laugh to make me blush. They were in their late teens or earlyish twenties. I could barely speak to girls. I was a bag of nerves in their presence and turned red at the slightest innuendo. One day I was upstairs in the storage area getting some tins for the shelves when one of them approached me near a pile of boxes. There was no-one else up there. We were alone. She was a gorgeous, sexy young woman with short blond hair, a beautiful face and all the equipment boys dreamt of. She cornered me and started asking me if I had a girlfriend etc. She had no doubt been put up to it by the other girls. I mumbled and shuffled around awkwardly. She came closer. I moved back but was trapped against a wall. As she continued with her sexy talk she pressed her hip into my groin and began to rotate it slowly. She had scent on and that, together with her natural odour, was intoxicating. I can smell her now, musty and warm ... Anyway her gyrations had the effect of getting me shall we say 'ready for action'. I was so embarrassed I could no longer speak. She then put her hand on my crotch and commented on my arousal asking if I'd take my trousers down and let her feel my ... well I was frozen in fear and confusion and wonderment. She said that men liked women to feel their manhood and I had no doubt whatsoever that she was right. Her lips were close to mine, her lovely breath breathing into my mouth. Her hand began undoing my belt buckle as she carried on whispering in her lovely seductive voice. Then we heard the

15

manager coming up the wooden stairs and she stopped what she was doing and we pretended to be working. That was over fifty years ago. At that time it was the most wonderful thing that had ever happened to me. I felt so happy. Looking back I feel so grateful for that beautiful girl's playful, sexy attention. She was gorgeous.

#12

I was a strange young man. Between the ages of fourteen and eighteen, when I had my first love affair, I was the coolest boy in Tonyrefail and as far as I knew the entire world. I was not like the others. They were vibrant and full of themselves, they were square-jawed and tough, I was a dandelion stalk in wire-rimmed glasses blowing in the summer breeze. My mind was filled with nameless fears and poetry. I acted the goat, no I was the goat, I was a drip, I was drip-fed. I talked in a language no-one understood. I hid beneath the overhanging branches, gazing out at the grey beauty. When I look back it pains me that some girl didn't spot me there and become my girlfriend. I would have been the best boyfriend in the world. We could have trod among forgotten ways; we could have climbed the strawberry mountain. Instead I wrote the book of heartache. Though I have had a quite wonderful romantic life I still feel I missed out somehow on what could have been in those delicate magical years. Young love is what I'm talking about. I may sound like an old fool here but I truly believe that the present day obsession with pornographic images that youngsters get bombarded with have sullied the beauty of naive adolescent relationships to the detriment of the young people and to the world as a whole. I am not against sex. Far from it and I am not against young people doing what comes naturally but I guess I'm against the premature despoilment of innocence. When I think of my missing years I think of the wonder of getting to know another person, a girl, and being let into her thoughts and dreams and ideas, of spending time together, of walking by the sea or along Pant y Brad on a Sunday evening. I think of holding hands, of laughing together and watching the twilight fall. I think of sex too, of course I do, but not just sex. Human relationships are the most important things in life. They are the point of it all. Love is all you need.

WALES

#13

When I was about seventeen me and my mate Steve, who was a couple of years older and wiser than me, went to Cardiff for the day. We had more than a few pints in the morning and in the afternoon decided to have a look around the big city. Steve always had an eye open for making a few quid and when we passed a shop window advertising 'Jackets for 7/6d' and trousers for three bob his eyes lit up. He figured that clothes were much cheaper in Cardiff and if we bought them in bulk, thirty Jackets and thirty trousers say, we could match them up and sell them as suits up in the valleys at a good profit. Cost 10/6d – sell at £1/10 shillings - a quid a suit profit!! Times thirty – thirty quid!! This was when I was earning eight quid a week. It sounded good. Steve went to a bank and got out the investment cash and we went into the shop. Steve asked the woman for thirty jackets and thirty trousers and put the money on the counter, the woman paused for a moment and said 'You do realise this is a dry cleaners, don't you love?' Steve will deny this story.

Last year, looking for something new to stimulate my jaded mind, I took up Snail Racing. Like many things that sound odd it is in fact great fun when you get into it. Another good thing is that I always win. Just kidding! No, it's snail versus snail. There are several clubs in the valleys and I attend The Boars Head Snail Racing Evening on the second Tuesday of every month in Tonyrefail. There are about forty members with snails of varying ability but in partnership with Liam, a snail I found eating my wallpaper a few months ago, a handsome chap with antlers like a bull moose, I immediately found myself in the prestigious second rank along with several regulars and a retired police officer named Fister. The first rank, the Lindford Christie of snail racing, is inhabited by Tom 'The Dreamer' Williams and Sid who to my knowledge have never been beaten. Tom has the advantage of course of having a huge private income and nothing else to do but train Sid, but that doesn't detract from their record. Anyway I was coming close, in the meet before last I was pipped at the post, so in order to try to give myself an edge I talked to some friends of mine in the aviation design industry and came to the conclusion that Liam's shell, being somewhat knotted, was a hindrance to his speed so I removed it, a painless and reversible procedure, for the next race. I believed that it would make him more aerodynamic, more speedy. But I was wrong. It had the opposite effect in fact, it made him more sluggish.

I was lying in bed in the early hours on Tuesday in Solva when I was woken by a pebble being tossed at the guesthouse room window. I got up, crossed the silent carpet floor, opened the cherry curtains and gazed out. There in the muted, lampshade glow of the streetlight stood Kevin Allen and several local fishermen all staring up at me as if I were a strange new star. The fishermen, bearded and clad in the filthy rags of their calling stood silent and dead eyed behind their master Kevin, who was dressed in luminous green swimming trunks new from Woolworth counters, flippers made from the skeletons of skate and Nazi tank commander goggles. Kevin told me that they were going down to the harbour to swim out to the flat sacrifice stone where pretty girls lay singing to the mermen. He wanted me to go with them. It sounded crazy to me and I said so. I told him it was two o'clock in the morning and that he should go home. He didn't seem to understand. I went back to bed and managed to fall into a sea tossed dreamless semi sleep. Later I had the strangest experience. I heard a noise, window latch lifted lightly footfalls ... then I was lifted in short strong arms and carried down a steep set of steps to the breeze of the salt air night. Then I was lifted high, held by many hands and carried in holy procession down certain winding streets and leaf strewn lanes to a beach, coved and gentled by the soft lapping of angel wing waves. Then out ... soft lifted rafted like a Woodbine packet cast away in moonlight love walk ... there listening to the dark crystal jewellery till come to rest on the stone hand of night. I lay there for minutes uncountable like time passed in a thought. Then the mournful singing of the fishermen in their deep, rhythmic coarse throated phlegm encrusted sad sadness of their loveless bed voices. Then Kevin dancing light footed among them,

'Look at my white arms boys dive deep with me' ... the laughter ... the slap of skin ... Valhalla Boys! I sank into unfathomable blackness. Only the faint distance of hands hauling me ... I woke the next morning bright as new life. What a dream ... but then a trail of seaweed ... damp impression of naked feet ... skate bone pattern there from my bed to the open window. I saw Kevin at breakfast. He said nothing. I have decided to let it go. No harm was done but I am wondering what I have let myself in for.

Amongst other things, Adolph Hitler destroyed the popularity of the then quite acceptable 'Charlie Chaplin' style moustache. This is a sad thing. Not that I'd wear one myself but there are, or should I say, *were* those with such an inclination. It was one of his lesser evils of course but still I think it deserves mention. A similar thing happened when I was a young lad living in Tonyrefail back in 1970 with the horrific Charles Manson murders. As well as the obvious, Manson made the sporting of a swastika tattoo on the forehead, previously regarded as the height of fashion among local young men, a symbol of psychotic mental derangement. Dozens of them were forced to scrub them off with bleach and ended up with unnatural sprawling sickly white scars on their foreheads in their place. Fortunately this was adopted as a new fashion by the local boys and little harm was done. Odd though and quite interesting these by-products of evil …

This reminds me … I was once at a gig/dance in a club up the valleys, it must have been 1969, and I was dancing drunk with an equally drunk young lady as the band pounded out their stuff. We were among a gaggle of other drunken dancing couples and hysteria reigned. There were a gang of mindless, semi-human thugs gathered pints in hand around the dance floor and the atmosphere was threatening and getting worse. As I spun around I caught a fleeting glimpse of a simple-minded yet nasty faced young gentleman who had for some reason zeroed in on my presence. As I whisked by spinning and twirling, illuminated by the flashing onstage lights as if on a fairground ride, he pointed at me, face aglow with hatred and animosity, and shouted out – 'I'm going to fucking kill you, you cunt!' The next time I spun past that spot he was gone. I never saw or heard from him again yet I can still see his face. The tendrils of human interaction are endlessly varied aren't they? In retrospect I quite like the guy.

I was at a football match, Cardiff City v Crystal Palace, in the late sixties and I noticed that every time the Palace winger got the ball the crowd would erupt, and I mean really erupt, in a sea of monkey noises. I'd heard this before but was bemused because the winger wasn't black. He was white! I asked an older person sitting next to me why this was happening. He said that what I took to be monkey noises was in fact the word 'Jew' repeated over and over very fast. The winger was the brilliant Mark Lazarus.

I was in a pub in Llantrisant on a Saturday evening in the eighties. I'd been rehearsing with Statues of Us all day upstairs but we'd finished and I went into the bar for a pint. The bar was packed to the rafters as people had crowded in to watch a boxing match between Colin Jones (I think) and an American. It was for a world title (I think). There was a strange, unpleasant atmosphere. The room was thick with cigarette smoke and there was a wild, pagan hysteria in the air. Over the course of the fight a mood of violent unhidden racism engulfed the audience. Men and women alike were screaming the most terrible abuse at the American fighter, a black guy, they were cheering when he began to bleed. They were calling him a monkey. 'Kill the black bastard!' It was like being in a side room in Hell. Human nature exposed at its most vile. I literally felt sick. I felt frightened. I felt terribly ashamed. I didn't say a word.

Cyril Regis died today. He was the first black footballer to play at the highest level in the UK. He was a brilliant footballer, big, tough and delightfully skilful. Praise to him. Love to him. Nice one Cyril ... Nice one!

I gave up smoking in 1978. Until then I, being a Welsh drunk and singer in a touring band, I smoked like the proverbial funeral pyre. I gave up because I had a scare. I was standing side of stage at The Milky Way in Amsterdam ready to go on with the band, The Lemmings, when I realised I couldn't breathe. It was weird. I thought 'Aye aye, this is it! I've destroyed my breathing apparatus with tar and such other shit and now its buggered and I'm going to die!'. The gig was terrible needless to say because although vocal technique was not my strong point I still needed to breathe a bit and I couldn't. I have never smoked a cigarette since ... no tobacco, no nicotine, no none of it. Giving up smoking is probably the best thing I have ever done in my life. I would have died by now had I not. Anyway I was walking up the street today headed for oblivion when I passed a man smoking a fag outside a poshish, modern pub. He was skulking in a slough of embarrassed despond as many of these modern day lepers do. The thing is, though I dislike tobacco and don't want to breathe it in second hand I felt a nostalgic empathy with the bloke. I thought of my younger days being brought up in Tonyrefail, the pubs full of working men relaxing with a few pints and a Woodbine or two. I have photographs of my old man sat with his friends, smiling, holding up their glasses, the air filled with curling smoke, the sunlight falling through the window, the smoke caught in its beams. There were joyous evenings spent in friendship and laughter. My old man was a typical Welshman. He liked a pint and a fag. Such simple pleasures would be denied to him today just as they are to the bloke I passed walking forlornly up and down outside the posh pub today. The posh menu written on a blackboard in the window seemed to mock the poor bugger. Ah ... it made me sad. I am a confetti of contradiction. I want the beauty you see. I want the love. But what I see is grey eyed hopelessness. I don't belong to these times. I don't desire the things the rest of the world seems to desire. I am the unhealthy face of desire. As you can see I am in a melancholic state today. It's not the black pit though. It's the teary dream of yesteryear. Thank the angels for such tender mercies. Love to you all. Boyd the Wurlitzer King. XX

#19

I was alone in the house, my mother and father had gone to London, to my Cousin Edna's wedding. She didn't want me there, we never got along. I was in bed. It must have been midnight or thereabouts. Anyway I was lying there in semi-sleep when I heard a floorboard creak on the landing. I opened my eyes. There was another creak, the muffled, scraping sound of footsteps approaching my door. Then they stopped. I turned my head and looked at the door handle, there was an ice cold terrible stillness ... then the handle began to turn ... slow ... strong and deliberate. I felt the blood trickling down my veins. I was unable to move ... and when the handle was fully turned there was a dreadful pause and I knew that whoever, whatever, it was standing there on the landing outside my door was thinking. That was the most horrible thing ... it was deliberating its next action, a heartless, dead logic was at work. Then the handle was loosened and ... and the thing shuffled away ... back to where it had come from. I knew what it was you see. Mister Pitt, the previous owner of the house, had lived on his own for many years after his wife's death. He had nursed her as she suffered the agonies and madness brought on by cancer of the brain. He held her hand throughout the final twilight. He became a recluse after she'd gone and his body wasn't discovered for many months after his own death. They say he died of starvation, deliberate starvation. It was him. It was his unsleeping tormented soul lingering on there in the house, in the attic with the trunks full of his wife's clothes and possessions where they found him. That was who it was paused in unhuman thought outside my door that night. That was when I realised that I was right to fear the darkness. I don't fear it now; I'd welcome the company now. At least his desires were plain, his motives uncomplicated. I'm not afraid of anything anymore. Let them do their damndest.

I was brought up in Tonyrefail, in the Rhondda, in the fifties and sixties. It was an intense and, in many ways, beautiful culture. Everyone was working class and our joys and dreams were drawn from the same well. The air smelled of romance, women and girls had sparkling eyes and men breathed out Woodbine smoke. Christmases glittered with fairy lights and falling snow. There was heartbreak and madness and violence of course, but I was a young man and the light outshone the darkness.

This was a country, a society, at a very particular time. It wasn't that long since the Second World War had ended. The valleys were thriving in its aftermath. There was work for everyone who wanted it. A lot of men worked in the mines, in Coedely Colliery, though back-breaking, it was well-paid and the very nature of the work created a camaraderie and interdependence that carried on into our social life. Friendships between families were tangible, practical realities. We holidayed together in Porthcawl, two weeks of monsoon rainfall in the caravan park in Happy Valley, days spent on Coney Beach or wandering around the fairground.

The churches were full. The melancholic sound of their bells added to the delicacy of the long Sunday evenings. Tragedies and comedies were shared. There was illness, of course. The sight of skeletal men, white as laundered sheets, leaning on a windowsill in the street, gasping for their breath was commonplace. Cancer was ever-present. Illnesses like diabetes and polio, one treatable, the other almost extinct now, were killers then. We even had a smallpox outbreak in 1961. I remember a house opposite Tonyrefail pictures being isolated; a blue mark painted on the front. The disease and illnesses just bound us closer together though. There but for the grace of God … we knew what it was like.

It seems to me that the air was different then – lighter, chiller, sharper, more exhilarating to breathe. The seasons were more distinct, the winters colder and darker, the summers hotter and more brilliant. The countryside was green and delicate. When I die I'd be happy to be buried on the Glyn Mountain, where I spent so many happy days playing with my friends Gwynne and Mel. I'd be happy to think of my soul resting there above the village. There was a mood, a feeling of timelessness that is impossible to describe. Many people had lived through the entire century. They kept the old ways alive.

We were isolated. It was a place out of time; and strange and beautiful for it. We didn't want to join in the race. The race, of course, came to us anyway – and change came unbidden. Television news, beamed into our homes by satellites, brought the worldwide social revolutions to our well-scrubbed doorsteps, and our strange little fairy world was swept away. I was a dreamer, a Grammar School hippy, I was the Poet Laureate of Despair, I was a dandelion growing in a back garden.

There were others like me. We saw a brave new world and we wanted to be a part of it. The old world was left to wither on the vine. It is strange then that that old world, that old Wales, should be with me to this day. That it has moulded me so, been so intrinsic to everything I have done since. This Wales is all but gone, all but forgotten. There are those still alive who share that distant memory and its ghost lingers on in our general psyche, but it grows ever fainter. It fades with every passing minute. I find myself kicking against the inevitable dying of that light. I hold it so close and deep in my heart that I cannot, and indeed do not, want to let it go. The new Wales is one of technology and fashion. It follows worldwide trends and sensibilities. It is a modern society keen to be accepted by the outside world on their terms. This isn't a bad thing but it is a homogenizing agent. Our uniqueness lies in our history and heritage. Don't rush into the brave new world too quickly without thought. Remember who we are. We don't need to seek the approbation of the outside world so desperately. We are a great, fascinating people living in a beautiful mystical land. Don't throw out *y baban* with the bathwater.

#21

This poem was specially written by Boyd Clack and Kirsten Jones to mark the hundredth anniversary of the Sengenedd mining disaster.

It was first performed by Kirsten Jones underground at Big Pit, Blaenavon, in South Wales at a commemorative concert for the National Museum of Wales in October 2012.

A MOTHER TO HER SON

You are not going down the mines
I've told you that before.
You have got a brain
And that's not what it's for.
It's for thinking not for crawling round
In tunnels in the dark;
You'll go to college like your brother.
Don't you break my heart.

I know that your Dad worked there
But he says the same.
He had no choice
But you have got a brain.
He was just thirteen-years-old
When his father took him down,
When he did his first shift,
When he first went underground.

He said that he felt 'like a man'
Down there with the 'boys'
But they were just children
Who'd packed away their toys

And taken up the pick
And the shovel and the lamp
To dig out the blackest, blackest coal
In the icy cold and damp.

They thought that they were men then
Because men toil and sweat
And drink beer by the bucketful
And smoke and swear and bet
But you look at your father now
He can't walk twenty feet
Without stopping, gasping for his breath
White as a laundered sheet

The earth has claimed too many.
It's not having you.
The world is at your fingertips
There's so much you could do.
You can live life and be happy
In the sunshine and the rain.
You can breathe in God's fresh air my son
Because you have got a brain.

By Boyd Clack & Kirsten Jones

I started working in Cardiff Marine Tax Office in 1968. It was there I met what I believed to be the first gay man I'd ever seen. His name was Francis, he was in his fifties and he was a Quentin Crisp lookalike down to the lilac rinse. He worked on his own in a filing storage area in an alcove off a corridor. The young blokes took the P and some were cruel but he withstood it stoically. Today is the fiftieth anniversary of the legalisation of homosexuality in Britain. Growing up in the valleys in the fifties and sixties there were no gay men or women probably. This didn't stop homophobia of course and it was rife. When I was a teenager an overtly gay bloke coming into a pub in Ton would have had a hammering. A few years after I met Francis I went to Australia to live. There I moved in a circle of young hippie mystical types several of whom were gay. Since then I have lived all over the world and met many gay people. I don't understand how anyone male, or female come to that, can be sexually attracted to the male body; it's beyond me. People are either loving and decent and honest and kind or they are not. Colour, race, religion, sexual preference, none of these things dictate a person's worth. Prejudice exists as an entity separated from the subject, i.e. Someone is prejudiced first then they find someone or something to hang that prejudice on. I have many gay friends and they are as we all are, individual beings, some are lovely good people, some are jerks. Gay people are not defined by being gay any more than I am defined by being handsome and cool. We are all sparks from the divine flame. I have male friends who I love like brothers, quite a few of them. I wish I'd been nicer to Francis. I wish I'd given him a hug and told him I was a friend. Fifty years! Salutations and love to my gay friends. Boyd (Ultra Masculine, Rugged yet Sensitive) Clack.

Met up with old friend Gwynne Price the other day. He's a strange bloke but I like him. He's highly intelligent. In a different context he could have achieved a lot but his failure to live up to his potential has left him both sad and bitter. I tried to explain that so called 'success' is 99% luck but the unsuccessful never accept that. They seem to want to punish themselves. Gwynne is not alone. He is a type not uncommon in the valleys. We choose to see ourselves in the worst possible light. It's to do with an inbuilt yet inexplicable belief that we are not worthy of achieving our dreams. I can say this because despite a certain amount of success in my career I remain one of these people. The lack of courage we feel is in itself an example of luck. Where we are born, the social/financial situation we are born into and the corresponding increase in opportunities in life, education, social contacts, levels of self-confidence/belief ditto. Life is random. Determined by chance. Being brilliant or talented doesn't mean anything if no-one ever knows about it. Thomas Gray knew this. Shakespeare knew it. Sophocles knew it. It makes me smile when I hear 'successful' people claim they deserve their success because they 'worked hard all their life' for it. Surely they must realise that for every 'successful' person who claims this there are hundreds of thousands of equally able people who have worked hard all their lives and ended up poor, alone and broken. I said all this to Gwynne but he didn't buy it. I'll be seeing him again no doubt. I wonder what has happened in his life since we last met.

Disturbing experience yesterday afternoon, I was walking along the sea front in Barry when I saw a man and a woman arguing. The argument soon became violent and he started knocking her about. I have had experience of intervening in such things before and been turned on by both the man and the woman, told to 'fuck off and mind my own business.' Still ... the guy was an ugly bugger with a big nose and the woman was no looker either. They were screaming out insults. A copper turned up and was forced to take out his truncheon. He scuffled with the man, who got the better of him, took his truncheon and started whacking him over the head with it. I forgot to mention that the woman was holding a baby. I was put on the spot and was about to involve myself when a huge alligator turned up and stole a string of sausages from the woman's shopping bag. It was surreal I tell you. There were children laughing ... candy floss stalls ... donkeys. It ended up with the bloke battering the copper unconscious using the baby as a club. It makes you wonder doesn't it.

#25

In the mid to late sixties me, Steve Dudley, Paul Davies, and his wife Sandra, used to drive up to The Lamb and Flag in Paul's fruit-and-veg van every Sunday evening in the summers when it stayed light till late. We'd drink Whitbread Tankard, or in my case Mackeson Fillups, eat cheese and onion rolls and crisps and play darts till chucking out time. We behaved like idiots a lot of the time, clowning about, standing on tables reciting poetry that kind of thing. We'd be pretty much plastered driving home and we'd sing Wild Rover and other songs at the top of our voices. We were innocent fellows though like all youngsters we thought ourselves sophisticated. I used to walk up there other times with Maldwyn Collier and some of the other football playing gang. The night would be similar but we'd have to walk home in the moonlight. We'd run over the fields some nights shouting and laughing in our drunken joy. These were times that have stayed with me to this day. My entire life has been moulded by my youth in Ton in the sixties. I haven't lived there for a long time now, hardly at all really, as an adult but Ton is always in my heart. It is my home.

I also have a crystal clear memory of walking up Cymer Hill drunk at one o'clock one winter's morning watching the snow falling from the black sky in the light of the street lamps. It was like being inside one of those little snow domes that had been shaken. I was wearing my beautiful green Afghan coat that they took off me in Sydney Airport. I had long hair and round John Lennon glasses. I must've looked so sweet and delicate. It brings tears to my eyes just thinking about it. A great French writer wrote the beautiful line *Mais ou sont les neiges d'antan?* – 'But where are the snows of yesteryear?'. Where is the beauty I saw as a child? Indeed.

ACTING

#26

I was thinking about when as a boy in the fifties, me and Gwynne Evans used to play snipers up the Glyn Mountain in the summer holidays. It struck me that playing is the same as acting, then I somehow remembered that I didn't think it was me, little Boyd, who was pretending to be a sniper, there was an intermediary. It was this 'other' me who was pretending. The other me was a strong and clever chap, with courage and an adventurous spirit, very different to the 'real' me, a frightened little creature, devoid of courage. I then related this to my profession as an actor and considered whether it was now the real me acting or another intermediary me, and if it could have any benefit in knowing the answer to this. I am still mulling. I once pretended to be Anthony Quayle acting a part in the dress rehearsal of a play. Though the director thought it 'odd', I felt a certain release through doing it. Is this an interesting thought or just demonic waffle designed to confuse and distract? Actors will talk about acting endlessly given someone to talk about it with, as will people immersed in most other things. I love it.

The world of television and film is the modern day equivalent of the medieval court. An ordinary human being has to be invited to attend, to be there amongst the lords and ladies, to catch a sight of the king possibly, to observe and by observing to share in the opulence. The music business, publishing, fashion, the same rule applies. If fortunate enough to be invited you have to play by their rules. You have to be respectful and only speak when spoken to. You have to be constantly aware that you are being done a huge favour and act accordingly. There was a time when few could even dream of the possibility but now in the world of reality television celebrity it has become the holy grail for many. Warhol's exploding plastic inevitable has become reality. The thing I'd like people to keep in mind though is that this modern 'court' is just as the old one was; a closed shop only for those of noble blood and that your visit is an anomaly. You are not one of them. They don't see you as an equal. You are kept around as long as you are entertaining and of some benefit to them but the camaraderie they offer is as fragile as a dandelion clock. The great advantage that 'they' have over us is that they always stick together. We can be separated from the herd and disposed of with ease. That's because we are desperate and frightened. Henry Ford was once asked if he feared socialism, the uprising of the workers, he replied that it didn't worry him one little bit because he always knew that if push came to shove he could pay one half of the workers to kill the other half. These people do not baulk at mass murder to protect what they have. That is what wars are, the powerful sacrificing masses of ordinary people to protect their power. The modern day 'court' of television and film is not that extreme but the same principle applies. You are unimportant, you are disposable. Don't kid yourself that it's a nice world. Then again as Nietzsche put it 'He who is not an eagle should not build his nest above the abyss.' Love to you all.

I had done no acting prior to my audition for the Welsh College of Music and Drama, so when I had to find two audition pieces I went to the library and wrote them out. I was living in a squat, so I couldn't take books out. For a classical piece, I remembered there was a speech that started 'Friends, Romans, countrymen ...' and I asked the librarian where it was from – *Julius Caesar*, of course. I found it, wrote it out and took it home to rehearse for the audition the following Monday. I had never done a speech or anything before, so I just pounded it into my head going over it night and day, whilst standing in the kitchen of the squat. The night before the audition I was standing there going over it, it was three a.m. and when I lumbered to the line "He was my friend, faithful and just to me", I suddenly found myself in floods of tears. He was all these bad things, ambitious, vain, yes but, he was 'faithful and just to me', a line so powerful and profound, a line so in-tune with the reality of the human condition as to render one speechless. The place it appears in the context of the drama is one of ringing intensity. I had read Shakespeare in school, of course – Richard II for 'O' levels – and had recited bits to my old man in the front room. But I'd never been struck, as I was then in that kitchen, as to the enormous, universal genius of the man.

Since then, having become a professional actor I have appeared in several excellent productions of his works – *Macbeth* at Leicester Haymarket; *A Midsummer Night's Dream* at St Steven's; *Hamlet* at the Young Vic; *Coriolanus* with the Berkoff company in The West Yorkshire playhouse – and have come to the full realisation of the depth and scope of the bard's genius. He was not of this earth. He was a conduit for the angels. To explore every facet of the human condition with such profound insight and to have expressed it in such beautiful language, to have created such drama, such humour, such truth is unique in literature. Tolstoy, Dickens and other novelists haven't ever reached his level. The nearest I have come to Shakespeare's work is that of Sophocles, whose *Oedipus Rex* and *Oedipus at Colonus* are works of similar greatness. But even he stands second to William Shakespeare. He has made the world a more interesting place. He has shown us the universality of human thought and emotion. I love him.

There is no greater experience, no more transcendental, than acting on stage. It is beautiful and I have never felt happier or, strangely enough, more involved with reality than there. It is impossible to describe. A great play, one of the classics, works like a machine. It carries the actors with it. You surrender to its power and beauty. That is what made it a classic in the first place. I have actually seen sparkling silver dust fly from my fingertips on stage. I have felt to depths I had never felt before. Yep, it's something else and I am immensely grateful to have had, and hopefully to continue to have, the opportunity and honour to ply my trade. I want to play Prospero and Shylock. Partake in the works of Ibsen, Chekhov and the other Russian greats. There are so many wonderful plays and parts to play. It's like being a child in a magical toy shop. Love to my fellow actors.

I love Peter Gabriel-era Genesis. I spent several years listening to the 'Supper's Ready' side of Foxtrot every night lying in bed waiting for the narcosis of sleep. The beautiful guitar intro of 'Horizons', followed by Gabriel's plaintive, ethereal voice – 'Walking across the sitting room I turned the television off ...' then the intense journey to the glorious 'New Jerusalem' ending. It's a wonderful piece of music, rivalling anything ever written in my opinion. Years later I was working at the National Theatre in London doing a play called 'Tectonic Plates' with the great Robert Lepage who cast me as Sir William Rees, a classical pianist on a wonderful watery set with a grand piano in a swimming pool, and as it happened Robert had been liaising with Gabriel to create the stage show for his then upcoming tour, and when I walked into the bar one night after a performance I went to join Robert and found that the short guy in the golden jacket who he was talking to was Gabriel. Robert introduced us and I nodded. We stood there for half an hour or so as they discussed technical and artistic details of the show and do you know, I was physically incapable of speech. I couldn't utter a sound. It was like meeting someone you know like a brother but they don't know you. It wasn't Star-struckness, it was sensory suspension. He seemed a really nice man and glanced at me several times to see if I wanted to join in the conversation but I couldn't even grin in response. 'Hey babe, your suppers ready for you. Hey babe, you know our love is true.' I nonetheless treasure those moments. Working for Lepage was a magical experience all round in fact. He's a unique artist and the company of French Canadians and some Jocks was excellent. We did the show in the National Theatre of Canada in Quebec too and made a film of it in Toronto directed by Peter Mettler. When you're actually in the throes of doing something wonderful it is nearly always the case that you don't realise at the time just how fantastic it is, this is true of so much. To relish the present is a gift denied to most of us. Falling in love, being in love, these are not banal things. These are the things that make life.

I was in Chicago in 1998 and being there I decided to see if I could find one of those bars where big time Mafia criminals hung out, just for the excitement, to tell my friends when I got home you understand. I asked the bellboy at the hotel and he told me to go to The Bucket of Blood on Maine Street. I got a taxi. It was a warm sultry evening. I got a drink, a Sangrilla and Red Bull, and took a seat near the entrance to the toilets. It wasn't difficult to spot the gangsters. They were all Italian looking with expensive suits and they laughed out loud en masse every few minutes. The barman told me that they were members of The Butcher Boys a gang led by Luigi 'The Meat Cleaver' Rossini. His soubriquet was eponymous. He was known to have personally murdered over a hundred rival criminals by chopping them to pieces with the implement. He had not arrived that evening and was possibly out of town on 'business'. I was about to leave when a beautiful large bosomed woman in a revealing dress sat next to me and said 'So you're English hu?' I explained that I was in fact Welsh and that made her laugh. She said she liked me and asked if I would buy her a drink. I got us both a Vodka and Mango juice. After several more drinks she asked me if I'd like to join her in her room. I said yes and she led me up a flight of stairs to a rather elegant apartment on the third floor. As I said she was a very attractive woman in her early forties probably and I, being a Welshman, was not reluctant when she began kissing and fondling me though in retrospect it was probably sexual harassment. We ended up in a huge bed with silk sheets. She was wild with sexual desire and I found it exhilarating to say the least. There was a ceiling mirror above the bed and watching her voluptuous body writhing in ecstasy as she straddled me was extremely erotic. This would be a tale to tell the boys when I returned to Tonyrefail!! About ten minutes into this wild lovemaking the door to the bedroom was kicked open and a man about my age in a sharp suit stood there in silhouette with a meat cleaver in his right hand. The woman whose name I had discovered was Gina leapt up out of the bed. 'Luigi!' she said, almost in tears and shaking with fear 'I thought you were out of town on business!' Luigi said 'Well I'm home.' Gina began collecting her underwear from the floor where she had flung it in her rush to engage in sexual congress and said 'This is my husband Luigi.' I was I might add embarrassingly still in a state of sexual arousal. Luigi told her shut up and get out of the room and that he would deal with her later. She left almost immediately. Luigi shut the door behind her and locked it with a key. I stood up out of the bed and began to tell him that I had no idea the woman was married and I was sorry to have made love to her. I said I would never have pursued the course of action if I had even suspected such a thing. He listened then began walking slowly towards me sharpening the blade of the meat cleaver on a carberundum stone held in his other hand. He had a twisted smile on his scarred face. He said 'You are not the first but I have my honour. Honour means everything to we Italians.' For some unknown reason my state of arousal became even more prominent as he got closer. I looked from the window. The stars had come out. I told him that I was a professional actor and he let me go.

I have never had a bad review for acting. In fact I've had very good, oftentimes excellent, reviews for my work in theatre and on screen. That is not to say I have never been sub-par in things. I have but there were no reviewers there on those nights for those shows. I say this to counter the old 'sour grapes' response to anything an actor or writer may say negative about anything or anyone in the business. 'Sour grapes' means jealousy. I am not or never have been jealous of any actor I have ever met for any reason. I don't see acting like that. Success is illogical in our trade. Jealousy would be equally illogical. Most all actors are aware that 'success' is 99% luck. I know fine actors who never work and average actors who are household names. Anyway my point is this ... when a reviewer singles out a performance for particular praise it is practically always the lead or one of the lead roles. If not, it is a minor role played flamboyantly with the aim of grabbing the limelight. This leaves the other actors, who are usually equally good in their subsidiary roles, feeling unappreciated. For Hamlet to be a good performance all the other roles need to be good too. As Mickey Rooney said 'There are no small parts just small actors.' An actor is not supposed to 'stand out' from the rest of the cast. An actor does what they do with honesty and to the best of their ability at that moment. I would just like to point this out to those not in the profession. Look at the production as a whole – don't just concentrate on the main parts. See how fine someone can do with one line or a non-speaking part even. Respect the actor. To my fellow actors I say I admire you all regardless of casting. We must respect each other or we will become little better than talentless, squabbling celebrities obsessed with being noticed and uninterested in the joy and beauty of our wonderful, giving art. Break a leg.

I was working in Solva in west Wales shooting *Under Milk Wood* a few years back. One night I decided to take a walk along the seafront. My friend Aneirin joined me. We left the town area and after an hour or so found ourselves on a moonlit beach. It was there that Aneirin pointed out a large metallic object that seemed to be hovering above us in the starless sky. No sooner had he done so than a beam of intense white light shot down from the object encircling us where we stood. I tried to speak but found myself unable to do so. Both Aneirin and myself were held by some unseen force and within a matter of seconds found ourselves sucked up by the cylinder of light and drawn into the body of the strange craft. I became frozen as if in a waking dream, unable to move or speak. The next thing I recall is coming back into consciousness strapped to silver metal tray contraption in a white room. I saw Aneirin strapped to a second tray next to me. We were both naked but for a white gown. I tried to turn my head but it was held in place by a metal collar. I called out to Aneirin but before he could respond three creatures appeared. They were around eight-feet-tall with long sinewy arms and legs, bulbous heads and huge unblinking eyes. They seemed to be investigating us, our bodies, with great interest. One of them poked me with a rod of some kind and they made an excited sniggering noise when I complained. Aneirin was crying by this time. I asked them who they were and why they had brought us to this place. One of them replied in a distorted voice that they were from the planet Orm and were on a mission investigating life forms on other planets. I asked what they intended to do with us and he said that their main interest was in the expelling of waste matter by different life forms and that they intended to probe our rectums with an artificial arm.

Aneirin became hysterical at this point and began to struggle against the metal bands that held him down. The two other beings were attracted by his gyrations and I watched as they proceeded to penetrate Aneirin's anus with the aforementioned 'arm', though it was more like a walking stick than an arm in my opinion. Aneirin screamed throughout the entire procedure especially when they twisted the instrument to get a clearer view. After an hour or so they finished with him and turned their attention to me. I told them that I was a professional actor and they let me go.

AFTERNOTE
Aneirin is a professional actor too but had failed to mention it. He took four days off work.

When writing comedy, you are wasting major time if you try to write what you think other people will find funny. All you can do is write what you find funny and trust that an audience will agree. I recently listened to a radio performance of *Satellite City* in 1994 and it reminded me of what a great experience those recordings were. There was a live audience and, though it was on the radio, it was brilliantly visual. As I was walking down the street today a snatch of dialogue from a radio show that never translated to TV came into my head. It was where Dai is depressed about his wife running off with Don, the brewery rep, and Randy convinces him it would help him if he could express his pain through an art form. A section of the dialogue goes like this:

Dai: I've writ a play Randy.

Randy: That's great Dai! What's it called?'

Dai: 'Never Trust a Woman,' Butt.

Randy: Really ... what's it about?

Dai: It's about a barman named Dai 'oo's wife, Rosalie 'er name is, runs off with a brewery rep named Don in 'is Ford Granada an' Dai develops a non-specific urinary tract infection that makes it hurt like hell when 'e pees.

Randy: It's autobiographical then Dai.

Dai: No, Randy. It's based on my own life, butt.

When this came into my head today I burst into laughter as I was walking along. As I say, you can only really write for yourself.

I was walking through Red Square in Moscow, a few years before the fall of the communist regime, when I saw a man get up from a bench leaving a brown envelope behind on the seat. I grabbed the envelope to rush after him but he'd gone. I was deliberating as to what to do when two old fashioned cars pulled up and a group of burly men in long coats jumped out, snatched the envelope out of my hand, bundled me into the back of one of the cars and drove off. I didn't know where they were taking me as I had been blindfolded with a bag over my head. The car reeked of vodka. About ten minutes later the car was driven into a courtyard and I was dragged out protesting and taken into a building, up several flights of stone stairs and flung into a cold room with a stone floor. I lay shivering on the floor for what seemed like hours then the door opened, my hands were tied and I was sat up in a chair. When they took the hood off I saw I was in a bare cell with just the chair and a single unshaded light bulb above. There were four men, all thick set and unsmiling. The fattest one stood behind me and broke wind. One stood to each side and the fourth, a thin, bald man with wire rimmed spectacles, stood in front. He asked about the envelope. I told him what had happened and asked if they knew the man who'd lost it. He said that the man had died under questioning not ten minutes before. He asked why I was in possession of the names of all of the Russian double agents in British Intelligence. I told him I wasn't aware that I was. He waved a sheet of paper in front of me and started to shout. He then spoke to the man to my right who took a cloth container from his inside pocket and opened it out to reveal what appeared to be some medical implements. The bald man told me I had one more chance to 'come clean' as he put it or the other man, who he referred to as 'the good doctor here', would take over the interrogation using 'less friendly methods'. I told him I was a professional actor and they let me go.

I am, as many of you will be aware, a professional actor and if there is one thing that gives me pleasure it is watching good acting, be it on TV, film or stage. I love it. I recently watched *Death by Innocence*, an Agatha Christie adaptation, on the box and was delighted to see not only good acting, but a uniform and nowadays unusual, to the point of being extinct, style of acting delivered with panache. I am referring to melodrama. This style died out in the late nineteenth century with the universal acceptance of naturalism with Stanislavski, Chekhov, Ibsen et. al., in the vanguard. Melodrama became embarrassingly old hat almost overnight. It had a faux revival in silent films where the exaggerated physicality, particularly in facial expression, lent itself to simple interpretation by audiences, but that was just a stay of execution. For those unsure of what melodrama entails, think about large emotions signalled both physically and vocally – the moustachioed twirling villains of the silent screen, the leering Lotharios, the terrified virgins tied to the railway tracks. It is non-naturalistic. There are other acting styles, Brechtian alienation appears naturalistic but rejects it in its theoretical approach, for example, and there were weird schools such as futurism and surrealism which owed more to melodrama than to naturalism, though naturalism was the accepted style of the time. Dario Fo borrowed freely from melodrama as did much of absurdist theatre, but nowadays it seems actors and directors are actually afraid of it lest it be interpreted by audiences as 'not good' or 'old fashioned' or god forbid 'silly'! I did a melodrama workshop in college based on *The Red Barn Murder* plays popular in America in the latter half of the nineteenth century and all I can say is I really enjoyed it. It was liberating and fun. I suppose one could see a Brechtian 'showing' rather than 'being' element to it if one wanted to over-analyse, but I'd prefer to just see it as fun. It was lovely to see it in a recent Agatha Christie adaptation. I particularly liked Jack, the son who got murdered in prison and the escaped lunatic who was his alibi. I realise I am in a small, almost non-existent, minority here but I don't care. Sorry to non-acting friends who must find this a bit boring but fellow actors and lovers of acting will know what I mean. Love to you all. 'Ha Ha Ha Ha! You will never catch me you fools!!!'

Getting a scene or two in an established TV series can be extremely daunting for an actor. The first few times it happened to me I'd only just started out in the business and didn't realise the nature of such things, the pace, the fact you don't get to rehearse, the alien atmosphere and the fact that sadly sometimes the regular actors can be cold and unthinking towards you, unkind even, so it can be a lonely and upsetting experience, frightening even. One job I did of this type was in a cop drama in London, two nice scenes but because of feeling alienated by the regulars I had problems. I was frightened. During lunchtime, I went to the canteen and had some sandwiches and tea then when the regs came in they all went and sat together at another table leaving me on my own at mine. They were laughing and clowning about and giving me a very cold shoulder. I felt terrible then one of the regulars came in late and said 'You want another coffee, Boyd?' I said yes and he got his food and two coffees and sat with me. We had a pleasant chat about nothing in particular and it made me feel a lot better. I remember this as a very kind and dignified act. Later when I was a regular in things, remembering how it is, I always made a point of doing everything I could to make guest actors feel as included and valued as I could. The actor who sat with me was Hywel Bennett. It was particularly nice because I held him in such high regard. In fact I believe him to be one of the very finest actors in a generation of very fine actors, Terence Stamp, Glenda Jackson, David Hemmings, David Warner, Julie Christie to name but a handful, the new breed of actors who came to the fore in the late fifties and sixties. I remember Hywel best from the Potter TV play *Where the Buffalos Roam,* as the eponymous 'Shelley' in the excellent comedy series written by my good friend Peter Tillbury, as the co lead with Hayley Mills in the truly classic film *The Family Way* (See this if you possibly can. It is a great film), from a film version of Orton's *Loot* and as Ricky Tarr in the wonderful *Tinker, Taylor, Soldier, Spy*. Years later Kirsten and I had the honour of working with him in an episode of *High Hopes* where he played Mam's wastrel brother Tom. I used to just stand and watch him at rehearsals. He was so brilliant. It gave me great joy to see a fellow actor of such great talent practising his trade close-up like that. He was polite but not particularly communicative. I believe that he'd had a problem with alcohol for some time and I have no doubt it would have been that which prevented him acquiring the work and the acclaim his talent undoubtedly deserved. He died aged 73, I believe. I will always remember him first as the one who sat with me in that canteen and then as the beautiful and brilliant young actor who lit up the sixties with his girlfriend Hayley Mills and called to me through the cinema screens 'Hey Boyd, I'm a young Welsh boy like you. You can do this mate. You only live once. Come on!' RIP Hywel and thank you for your inspiration and kindness.

I can travel through time. It is something I've been able to do since I was a child but I cannot control where I travel to or what year it is. It is pot luck. For this reason I rarely do it as I don't wish to place myself in unnecessary danger. The last time I travelled I found myself in a room in an old building. I soon realised that it was a basement, a dungeon in fact. There were several other men there, one of whom spoke English. He told me that this was a monastery in Spain in the year 1512. The other men were emaciated and dressed in rags. I asked him why we were there but before he could reply the heavy door was opened with jangling keys and sliding bolts and a group of men, some in religious garb and some obviously soldiers entered. The other prisoners cowered but I, being new and somewhat naive, approached them and demanded to know what was going on. The leader, a thin-faced priest in a black skullcap, told me to sit down on a wooden stool. I did so. He then told me that he was going to put 'The Question' to me and if I answered truthfully, all would be well. This sounded reasonable so I told him to go ahead as I wished to get out of the oppressive place ASAP. 'Do you believe in the reality of transubstantiation during Holy Communion as described in the Holy Bible?' That was 'The Question'. I told him that I didn't understand it. He rephrased for my benefit. 'Do you believe that the bread and wine literally becomes the flesh and blood of Christ in the ceremony of Holy Communion?' I recalled something involving a bit of bread or wafer and a sip from a goblet of wine from my church days. The vicar would walk along giving them to the people who went up front as they knelt in a line in front of him. He'd mutter something too, something unintelligible. I asked the priest if this was what he was talking about and he confirmed that it was.

By now I had forgotten what 'The Question' was so he repeated it. I said I didn't see how a piece of bread could actually become the flesh of someone who died many hundreds of years before and ditto the blood/wine thing. Everyone in the room, soldiers, priests and fellow prisoners gasped in unison. 'So you deny transubstantiation?' the priest said. 'I don't "deny" it as such.' I replied 'I just think it unlikely. Why? Do you believe it?' The communal gasp was repeated. 'I know it to be the case,' he said. 'Fair enough,' I said 'Can I go now?' 'You will never leave here heretic. You will die here!' he replied. 'Die!? But why, what for?' 'For denying the reality of transubstantiation. It is a sacrilege,' he replied. I didn't want to argue or antagonise him so I said 'Oh … OK then I do believe it!' But then he called me a black-hearted servant of the Antichrist and said that I was lying to save myself having to suffer the agonies of the rack, which I now realised was the wooden thing like a large table football in the far corner of the room. I said I didn't know what to say because I'd said I thought it unlikely and that I believed in it so the only other thing I could say was that I didn't believe in it and I had a strong feeling that that wouldn't make him happy either. He then said that I can't merely 'say' anything, but that I had to 'believe' it to the depths of my eternal soul. I told him I did believe it to the depths of my eternal soul but he was having none of it. I decided on another tack. 'Look the truth is I'm not actually a Christian at all,' I said. 'I only ever went to church as a child and I had no choice in that. I was in the choir you see. All the other boys had no choice either. As soon as I became an adult I realised all that God stuff was rubbish, a fairy tale more or less. I mean … come on.' This time there was no gasp just a stunned silence. 'Bind him to the Instrument of Truth,' the priest barked and several of the soldiers lifted me bodily, took me over to what I now knew to be the rack, and tied my wrists and ankles to it with leather thongs. I was getting concerned. Then it struck me ... Spain ... 1512 ... The Spanish Inquisition!! I hadn't expected that. 'Hey I'm sorry, listen, I realise the mistake here now. You are Catholics right, Roman Catholics? Well I went to The Church of Wales! St David's in Tonyrefail. We didn't "believe" in anything. It was just somewhere we went. Your Catholic stuff has nothing to do with us, with me. My father told me it was heathen Dago gibberish! I gave a little chuckle. 'Begin the torture!' 'No! No listen ...' 'Turn the rack!' one of the soldiers began to turn the cogged wooden wheel where the corner flag would have been if the table had been for table football as I had originally thought. I felt the ropes beginning to tighten ... I was terrified ... What could I do to escape this hellish situation? What could I say?

AFTERNOTE

At the last split instant as I felt the sinews in my underarms begin to snap I cried out 'I am a professional actor!' and he let me go.

AGEING

#38

Saw my face in the window and I looked so old. It's strange. Hidden there in the aged flesh I can still see the sparkly eyed child, the young fresh-faced boy, awash with dreams, staring out. I can see the ghost of my own youth. Time passes. In every house the clock ticks relentlessly towards midnight. I don't mind getting old. In fact I quite like it. I'm not afraid of death but I am sometimes overwhelmed by the strangeness of having lived – all the loves and fears and arrogance and joys and regrets. My body is creaking to a halt like a huge ship braking in the middle of an ocean, time is slowing down and one day I will breathe out never to breathe in again and the ship will stop. I wonder if I will ever know anything. Will I ever experience anything in its pure form? You are the same as me. It's why I can speak to you without fear. Maybe we'll all become one thing in some unknowable afterlife. I will try to find something out before I die. If I do I'll share it with you. I seek knowledge through art but it is not in my hands.

Boyd Clack, The Poet Laureate of Despair

I realised today that I live in an almost permanent state of nostalgic melancholy. I dream of my younger days, till I was twenty essentially, and these dreams, memories, call them what you will, have come to supersede my present waking life. I recall practical things such as friendships, experiences, incidents, etc. and these invoke the atmospheres and moods of the time. A lot of it is grey and wintry. It is not uncommon for people to feel that they are living in the wrong era. I have discussed it with friends and acquaintances and many of them do so. The present world isn't my world. I don't relate to its values. I don't want any of it. I relate to Europe between 1900 and 1970. Probably Canada and Australia in those times too. The great European artistic movements of the early century, Dada, Futurism, the Bauhaus, the gloomy post-Gothic poetry and literature of the inter-war years. I relate to the delicate decadence. The political tumult was brutal but clear. It mattered which side you chose. Today it doesn't really matter. I love the English literature between 1920 and 1950, the plays, Rattigan in particular, the wonderful novelists, Lawrence, Waugh and Orwell. I feel the atmospheres of those long hot summers and bleak winters. I love the contemporary fashions, the suits, the shirts, the shoes and overcoats, the haircuts. Women's fashions were just so darn sexy, not just sexy though I find them romantic. Don't get me started on suspender belts! Whoever invented tights needed shooting. I was alive in the fifties and sixties, but too young to experience the subtleties of life. The second half of the sixties is the only time I felt I was in the right time. Yes, nostalgic melancholia for times I never lived in – that's my controlling emotion. Ah well it'll all be gone soon enough, I suppose. 'In the wink of an eye,' as they say. Life passes. Becket puts it beautifully in Godot:

'We give birth astride a grave. The light gleams an instant and is gone.' Maybe I'll be reborn in the bygone era. I hanker for in this. I can but hope. Love Sebastian Fflyte.

My birthday! When me old man had his birthday he always used to say 'Fifty five (or whatever) years since the blackest day in history!' I remember my old man a few weeks before he died telling me that he could remember playing with the horses up on Mynachdy farm with his brother in 1918 better than he remembered last week. I think about him and Naine, my mother, my sister Audrey, my brother Brian all gone and I wonder about it all. I don't know if there's anything remains of them or will be of me other than in the memories of the living but I don't think it really matters. Whether there is a god or a devil, heaven or hell, something or nothing, none of it makes any difference. We live, we revel in our youth, we dream, we play, we love, we ride the emotional roller coaster, we try, we fail, we reach for our desires but in the end we breath out and then never breath in again and become what the dead become. It's an extremely comforting thought. We join the eternal, oh so cruel chain or maybe it's a chain of delicate flowers. We flow back into The River of Souls and all the great dramas of life become as nothing. I see my death quite clearly, lying in bed in my bedroom, late summer afternoon or a winter day with a grey sky, rain falling heavily on my window, my friends have come, we have said goodbye, told each other that we love one another, recalled moments, laughed and cried and they have gone. My room is silent. My beloved sits nearby. If there is an after then we will be together again. Will my family, the ones who have gone before be there, stood as spirits around me? Will I see faces that I loved open-eyed and welcoming once again? I embrace whatever is to come. I have loved and that has made my life a good thing. I never wanted more. Well maybe a little when I was young and beguiled by shiny things but not for a long time now. I think I know what matters. I have done some stupid, unthinking and bad things but I can honestly say I have never consciously sought to cause any harm, pain or sadness to another being human or beast. I am a fool it's undeniable but I don't see that as a negative thing. Anyway, just a few thoughts on the occasion of this my birthday. Still a few years of maudlin introspection left I've no doubt. I would like to do some worthwhile serious acting in this time and I still feel there's some worthwhile, maybe even significant literary possibilities left. I have my beloved Kirsten to be the companion to my riper years and we enjoy a strange happiness most of the time. I love her. I love my cats too, each and every one of the gentle little souls. Life could be worse! There, I've said it!!!!! Don't expect me to ever say it again. I've got my reputation to think of! Love to you all.

MY FRIENDS THE TREES

When I die, bury me beneath the boughs of an old tree
no coffin
just what is left of me
and there my dust can mingle
with the roots of my ancient friend
deep inside god's earth
into everything again
into the falling rain
into the endless stars
no distance or separation
between what we were and what we are.

I was just thinking of when I was thirteen and heard the Beatles first album. I thought of John's beautiful voice, the great American Girl group numbers, the raw jangly playing. It made me cry, not just for the music but for the world then, how comparatively innocent it was, we were, I was. I wanted a girl to hug and kiss. I wanted to fly off into the sky. It made me wonder is this how I see the world, how I explain it or is it how I explain myself, what I have become. There are many people who devote their lives to the care, love and service of others. People who teach disturbed children, people who travel abroad to help the poor and hungry in those countries, nurses, doctors, aid workers, people who devote their lives to the protection of animals. Maybe I am ashamed that I have led such a self-absorbed existence and this is why I see the world through Kai's eye with the splinter of ice. I don't know. What I do know is that I should balance up my sad vision with the truth that I respect and love most everyone. I admire people for their bravery and kindness. The majority of people are flawed but beautiful. Indeed beauty doesn't exist without flaw just as courage doesn't exist without fear. I talk of the monsters outside but it is the monster inside that horrifies me. I am getting on in years and the clock is ticking as it inevitably does toward midnight. I am not afraid. I would like to leave some trail of goodness and decency behind but sometimes I feel so weak, so foolish that I fear that that is all that might remain. You know, I often feel so overwhelmed by the dignity and decency of my fellow human beings that it is unbearable, like I have no skin and all my nerve endings are exposed burning and crushed beneath the weight of the air. These thoughts and feelings are the source of depression. I would not like you my friends to think that my bleak mind blinds me to the intricate and divine truth that I live amongst angels. My personal pain thrusts the ugly in my face but the me underneath is always aware of the beauty. You are heroes one and all and my respect, love and admiration for you is a constant. Boyd XXX

I would point out that I am not afraid of death or dying. Obviously it would be nicer not to have to go through physical agony first but we have no choice as to how it comes so ... Interestingly I have a benign image of passing, actually dying itself I mean. I see a damp autumn evening, Sunday probably, I am lying in my bed with the twilight dimming the sky. I would hope to have one or two of my beloved cats lying with or near me. I would like to hear them breathing, the little snoring noises they make in their sleep. Possibly because of my Welsh Christian upbringing I actually find our rituals of death to be quite beautiful and profound. The idea that your friends and loved ones visit you in the final days, that they sit with you and hold your hand, that you can exchange farewells and talk openly and honestly about what you have meant to each other, that they kiss you one final time. All of that seems holy and right to me. I am enormously fortunate in having more than my fair share of real friends, people I love and trust completely. As you know my after-death belief is that of returning to the River of Souls where all life merges once again and flows throughout eternity. I love the thought of animals' souls mingling with ours as I know that they will, that they do. God is everything in my opinion and by that I mean literally everything. That is why god is omnipresent, why god is endlessly forgiving and accepting. Anyway, the negatives of death are there of course, no longer moving in the physical plane, being within the natural world of weather and seas and mountains, no more listening to the beauty of music, birdsong, Mahler, Floyd ... no more laughter of children ... these things I will miss and of course the fact that those I love, especially my sweetheart and loving companion KJ will be sad and miss me. This is painful to contemplate but we are all going to die, we all take our turn on the wheel and we will be together again I know this. I know that there are those who fear death. I cannot understand this. I am not saying we should seek death out or try to hurry it along but when the time comes, we are making ourselves whole, finishing the story. Surely this is the greatest experience of our lives. Don't be afraid. On his deathbed Thomas Hobbes, the great philosopher said ... 'Now I am about to take my last voyage, a great leap in the dark.' He and Marlon Brando and Queen Elizabeth the First and Leo Tolstoy and ... you get my drift. Love to you all and love to all of those I have loved who have gone ahead. I think of you and my love for you will never die ... can never die. Like I say there is no need, indeed no sense or point in fearing death. Love life.

MY OLD MAN

I sat on a chair at the side of the bed
Where my old man was lying dead
The world was silent
His skin was white
I touched his face
In the dead morning light
Once, years before, I'd been insane
Lying in bed with my then wife Jane
And in the dead of the night
I heard him cry out my name
His heart had been hurt
And I was to blame
Once, years before, he'd lifted me
Up on his shoulders for the whole world to see
I was the commander
Of a ship on the sea
And he was the ocean
That carried me.
I lay down by his side
And held him tight
As he had held me
All of my life.
I said
'Sweet dreams old man
Good night, good night'
And I kissed his sweet soul
As it took flight.

ANIMAL FRIENDS

#45

Watching Attenborough's new doc on the Beeb, a scene shows a family of elephants, two generations of females plus a brood of little ones, waking up and trekking across a plain. They came across the bleached bones of a dead elephant in the wilderness and a reverent aura descended on them one and all. They went up to them and explored them delicately with the ends of their trunks. It was a still evening, each did it in turn while the others nestled close to the one doing it, resting their heads lightly on one another. Even the babies knew that something special was taking place. These beautiful creatures were evidently in touch with the historical link they had with the dead of their species. They were honouring the sacred quality of ancestry, they love, they are aware of the continuity of their being. Surely this is by definition the possession of what we think of as a soul. How can we humans fail to see the divinity in our fellow creatures? It suggests wilful blindness to me. Are we too ashamed? Do we harbour the guilt of our barbarism towards them? We are belittled by this. Incidentally I speak of creatures, such as elephants, where the possession of a soul is inarguable but there are other living things – those that scuttle and crawl, those that cling to a spot and never move, those that glow in the ocean's depths – where it is not so obvious. I maintain that soul or not, these little ones are just as worthy of our love, protection, and respect. Maybe they are so close to the infinite that they don't need souls. I have on occasion been called a nutter because of my unwavering love of all creatures. I am a hideous hypocrite, of that there is no doubt, and I despair at my own weakness but I never waver. Bury me in an apple orchard that I might taste your lips again. Love Boyd of Assisi!

Song of The Mother Vixen

Oh my dear autumn is dying.
Autumn is dying and winter is here.
And the leaves on the trees are all dead or dying
And the wind through the valley is chill with my fear.

For who shall come feed us? Who'll give us shelter?
When the snow's on the ground and the flowers are dead?
Who will we turn to in the blackness of night time?
When the cold wind is blowing and we don't have a bed.

We'll have to huddle together in bracken
Hide from the rain in the old ruined barn.
I am afraid that bad things will happen
To me and my babies: that they'll come to harm.

Pray to the white sky. Pray to the river.
Take us and hold us in your kindly embrace
Have pity on a mother and help her deliver
Her little children from this barren place.

For who shall come feed us? Who'll give us shelter?
When the snow's on the ground and the flowers are dead.
Who will we turn to in the blackness of night time
When the ice wind is blowing and we don't have a bed.

#47

Sitting by the light of my desk lamp with my angel Almond on the desk next to me. She is watching what I do intently. It must seem inexplicable to her pure and perfect little mind. I am her daddy though and she knows I love her so she accepts my strangeness with grace. One day our atoms will mingle in the infinite universe and we will be as one. In my eyes this is the most glorious, most desired outcome to the black comedy of life. I can't wait. I just kissed her on her pretty little nose. She smells like a garden in ancient Persia. Love her to bits. Any of you my friends who are unhappy, stressed, broken even, please know that the company of, and physical contact with, our animal brothers and sisters is a sure pathway to peace and the soothing of anguish. Their innocent beauty enters into us by proximity. Beautiful music too ... Mahler's 4th and 5th symphonies late at night lying in bed in the darkness ... the religious choral music of the middle ages ... 'Supper's Ready' ... We must try to take care of our hearts and souls. We must be kind to ourselves. We must see the perfection at our core. It is there. I often don't see it. I see only the barbed wire and leprous scarred face in the mirror but I do know that there is the child beneath, the child which like the beasts is perfect and undefiled.

#48

I found a fly floating in the cat's water bowl this morning and scooped it out. I thought it was dead at first but noticed some flickers of movement so I let it rest on the palm of my hand. The flickers slowly increased and eventually the little wings began a tentative fluttering and from there the tiny being began licking itself and exploring with its little nozzle. It came back to life in my hand and I put it on the window ledge outside to complete its Lazarus-like resurrection. It was clear to me in those moments looking at that fly recovering that it was one of God's children and even though apparently so alien to me in its relationship to our environment and its conduct we shared a commonality of being as strong as any. I don't regard myself as inherently superior to anyone or anything in this world. We are different but equal in my eyes. I was touched by the little creature's beauty and innocence. Live for a day, live for a century, in desert, forest, city or dustbin, life is life. Love Boyd (St Francis) Clack.

#49

I have decided that we humans have been getting the wrong end of the stick for too long and I intend to balance things up a bit. Here is what I have done so far in this regard:

I kidnapped a Martian and stuck an electric probe up its arse; at least I think it was its arse.

I went to the zoo and masturbated openly in front of a family of chimpanzees.

I threw a handful of my own shit at a baboon while I was there.

An exhilarating experience!

AND next week I intend to find an old house inhabited by ghosts, move secretly and uninvited into the attic and then wander around, moving things about and making little noises in the nights when they are asleep.

This is my plan and I am taking the opportunity to encourage other humans to make similar gestures. What about leaping out from behind a bush and frightening a bear for instance (if you live in Canada that is) or scuttling across the floor unexpectedly and giving a spider a shock. I'm sure you will think of things. Follow a werewolf through a dark forest always keeping just out of sight. Watch as he or she stops, pauses, and looks back every ten seconds or so. Hee hee hee! It's time we put the boot on the other foot. We can call ourselves the Human Liberation Front.

#50

I was listening to a bird, a single bird on a rooftop, singing as I walked to the coffee shop this morning. It was so beautiful, a music more delicate, more ethereal, than any created by humankind. It made me think about death. What would I miss? Well, high up on the list, probably at the top of the list would be the divinity of nature, the beauty, the majesty of the physical world. There is so much that still takes the breath away: the landscapes, forests, fields, mountains purple in the distance, the seas, the streams, the babbling brooks, the mists of bygone mornings, the gentle hues of a thousand sunsets, the sky, sparkling blue and filled with diamond stars, then the creatures we share this Eden with, the creatures of the sky soaring in their majesty, the twirling, glittering fish with their myriad colours, their massed minds acting out their intricate dances, and the flowers and plants, the weather, rain, sun and snow, the wind, the clouds, the deserts and jungles, the animals, humbling in their perfection. All of them, all beautiful, all unsullied by evil: the tree beasts, the crawling ones, the flying, swimming, burrowing, running, hopping, slithering, scurrying ones, all endlessly loveable. We humans have forgotten what really matters. Our days and nights are spent torturing ourselves with the unimportant, our values are skewered by our artificial desires, our sense of beauty disfigured by fashion and greed. It's sad. Listen to the birds singing. We will all die one day, the pity of it is that so many of us would not have truly lived.

#51

Was sitting on the sea wall the light the bluish white of showered sky, the water greyish green, looking at the wooded hill on the far side of the estuary, seagulls flew past low above my head crying out, looking for tiny fish or discarded chips. Lovely creatures they are. I imagined the foxes and weasels and lizards moving in the woods.

I wondered whether I was as loved by God as they. I felt loved at that moment. I felt at one with the beauteous land and the gentle sea. I felt my soul was in harmony with the beasts. The same wind caressed us. The same sun bathed us. This is the magic hidden behind the synthetic noise. Simplicity!

I got married several years ago. My bride's name is Lottie Lotkins of Lotkins Hall. The ceremony was held in a farmyard near Tonyrefail and was conducted by the farmer. All of the ducks, geese, sheep, cows and horses attended and there were little pig bridesmaids, lovely they looked to with their garlands of buttercups and shiny snouts. The best man was Pippin, a handsome black and white fellow who lives with us. The reception was held in the grounds of Lotkins Hall. There was a buffet with fish, cream and various cold meats followed by games such as running up and down the lawn, hiding in three bushes and rolling on our backs. We partied till sunset then all fell asleep lying around on settees and carpets. It was a lovely day. Our marriage is a platonic one of course. Lottie loves me but not in that way. My human form, though she has grown used to it over the years, is nonetheless instinctively repulsive to her. I accept this readily as she herself, though unspeakably beautiful, does not attract me in a carnal way either. We are of different species you see. I love her beauty, her divine, radiant face, her soft silky fur, her four legs, her loving and gentile character and her angelic nose; she loves my ability to almost magically conjure up food and to rub her on top of her head and under her little chin where she herself cannot reach. We have never had a cross word. She chastises me occasionally with a swipe to the nose but her claws, razor sharp and deadly to birds and small rodents, are never out of their sheaths when she does so. It is a slap, not a punch, and she only does it when I deserve it. I have never loved any living creature more than I love her and she reciprocates with a degree of tenderness and kind attention that fills my heart with gratitude. She's never let me down in any way. I often find her lying next to me when I wake in the mornings and I am always happy to see her and feel her there. She snores a bit but it's a gentle, pretty sound, very ladylike and I find it relaxing and sweet rather than annoying. Oh yes, her smell! Musky and warm, sometimes a little fishy or grassy, always heavenly. I know we'll be together for all time. I am the happiest man on earth for that. She raises me from my foolish, introspective gloom. She is often my saviour. I love her. Thank you Potkins.

POP CULTURE

My pet rat Elvis died this morning. He was caught in a trap. Talking about pop music I was contemplating the question 'What is the greatest pop single of all time?' I'm sure we all have our opinions. I love singles from the sixties and there are a plethora of great ones – 'MacArthur Park', 'Wichita Lineman', 'Man of the World', 'Strawberry Fields', 'Waterloo Sunset', 'All or Nothing', the list is virtually endless so to edit it down I contemplated the bare bones of a great pop song. The classic and best subject is romantic/boy and girl/ lustful love, sex in fact, teenage sex. That doesn't cut many from the list of possibilities. So let's look at their components:

A classic musical hook, normally the chorus or a guitar line (Every Time that You Walk in the Room).

Then there is the overriding idea, bitterness turned to sorrow, longing, unrequited desire, etc. Beyond this is the idea, the concept, rare and wonderful when first done often becoming cliché with impersonation and time.

And finally the capturing of the moment, the zeitgeist if you will. 'See Emily Play' and 'Starman' are perfect examples.

Anyway – the one I've chosen is played by the greatest group of all time, sung by the greatest singers, contains two of the greatest vocal hooks of all time, captures the moment to perfection and has a simple but incredibly clever hook concept – that of using the second person in a way that every schoolboy is familiar with – all packaged into a worldwide number one hit. The band: The Beatles. The Singers: Lennon and McCartney: The vocal hooks – 'Yeah Yeah Yeah' and 'OOOOOOH', The Moment: the early sixties. The Hook Concept as stated above AND, the magical touch: it says the words that every boy in the world wanted and still wants to hear. The Song: 'She Loves

You.' All hail the Beatles, the defining voice of the sixties, the greatest band ever. (Floyd a close second.)

PS The list is endless, though I would like to point out that the remit is greatest ever POP SINGLE, not the greatest song.

#54

I saw *Jaws 3* last night. Now I think we all agree that Jaws was a great film and book. The thing is that it doesn't take Stephen Hawking to figure out there is a sure-fire way of avoiding shark attacks. KEEP AWAY FROM THE FUCKING WATER! Right? In Jaws 3 a woman whose husband was torn apart by a great white in *Jaws 2* is crippled by the trauma so she decides to go away on holiday to recuperate. Where does she go? A beach hut in Barbados!! When there, despite her trauma, she decides it would be good therapy to swim every chance she gets. It's ludicrous. You cannot help but root for the shark. The woman deserves to be eaten alive. I felt like leaping up and shouting 'Stay away from the water you daft bat!' like other people in the cinema did but ... seems that Americans simply cannot restrain themselves from swimming in the sea. It's like owning guns: a right they must utilise. You could tell them a tanker had spilled ten thousand gallons of sulphuric acid into the water a mile out from the shore, and they'd still grin and say 'Gee' and wade off into the surf, their legs melting into skeletal bone. It is demented. Ah well, as I said a small point but I feel better for getting it off my chest. Off for a dip now.

#55

There was a TV programme on the other night called *Wanking the Dead*. I put it on and at first it seemed promising. There was a dead body, a young woman, laid out on a trolley in a police morgue. The set up was perfect but though I watched eagle-eyed for the entire hour there was no post mortem masturbation in it whatsoever. On rechecking the TV book I realised that I had misread the title. It was in fact a standard detective type series called 'Waking' the Dead, a simple mistake to make. I was disappointed. I was really looking forward to the misread version. The thing is I think a show called *Wanking the Dead* would be very popular. It would attract huge audiences. In Wales it would anyway. Evenings would be planned around it. I'm not suggesting that corpses should just be grabbed willy-nilly for the purpose, though I'm sure they wouldn't mind, they'd be dead, but people could give their permission before they die, like with organ donation cards. There'd be none of this 'Opting out' rubbish either. It would have to be a definite 'Yes'. They could get B-grade celebrities to do the actual business, Joe Pasquale maybe or Patrick Moore. Maybe Dame Vera Lynn would acquiesce. It could be a new direction for her. Ex-sportsmen would be queuing up. They'll do anything for money or to be on TV. They could have a Welsh speaking version, not that it would have much actual dialogue but they could call it simply *Y Wankio*! Anyway, I've sent the idea to HTV and they said they'd get back to me. I'll keep you informed as to its progress.

It's unimportant I know but I feel that I must voice my disappointment, nay disillusionment with the new Doctor Who, and by 'new' I mean all of it, the revival of these last ten years or whatever. I was a fan of the show since the William Hartnell days and, though never a fanatic, enjoyed it a lot. The thing is Doctor Who should be an elderly eccentric with white hair and an unworldly air, not some handsome young chap who women fancy. It's ludicrous. It happens all too often these days and it's down to the yanks of course. They cannot conceive of interest in a character that is not linked to sexual attraction. Indeed their remakes of the Mrs. Marples stories, now in production, stars a young hottie in the title role. They take from the old every vestige of self-respect. They cast us out of our rightful place and replace us with advertising fodder. We are not to be seen. I speak as the only Welshman to have played the eponymous Doctor (The Celluloid World of Desmond Rezillo – Dr. 'OO). Also when I was in drama college I used to go about in a long army greatcoat, a long scarf and a small gold and black suitcase and there was not a single person who was not absolutely sure that I would play the Doctor in any future revival and they were right to be so convinced. Ask anyone. I mean it's a no-brainer isn't it? I was born to play the part and yet in this new incarnation there would be more chance of Damon Albarn getting the call. I feel sorry not for myself, I am a big boy I can take it, but for the viewing public who have to watch the glossy shiny-toothed parody they are presented with and pretend to think it's acceptable. The poor dears missing out on ME! I'd be the greatest doctor ever. As well as all the classic qualities, I'd add the slight but significant idiosyncrasy of being as cool as hell. I'd be the hippie doctor, the psychedelic time traveller sailing the flower strewn oceans of infinite time and space. It's a disgrace that I have not been offered the chance. Love to you all.

DECORUM

I have never been a slave to fashion. I go along with Quentin Crisp's assertion that fashion is the antithesis of style. It seems obvious to me. Fashion is a mass movement whereas style is individual. It is impossible for a Fashionista (horrific new word!) to have style. They are followers by inclination. Style or 'cool', as we now call it, is inherent. It's not to do with what you wear. It is a variation of charisma. A 'cool' person would look cool in a duffel coat and flares. An uncool person would be uninteresting in an Armani suit. Take this ripped jeans thing for example. You see multi-millionaire actors and pop stars wearing them. Why? Well they want to suggest that despite the image of being the modern gods and goddesses that they spend their lives cultivating, they are also 'down with the people', that they still have a link with the world of the despairing. Other people wear the torn jeans to show the opposite, that despite being poor and unknown they are still a part of the world of glamour and celebrity to which they have been taught to aspire. What a convoluted affectation! The haves and the have-nots meeting in the slashed denim of desire. I am qualified to speak on this subject because I am one of those blessed with natural, unshakeable cool. If I walk into a room full of the Glitterati (Yes I know) at an awards ceremony or into a valleys pub at ten o'clock at night I am always the coolest person there. It's always been the case. Everyone who knows me knows this to be true. I remember discussing it with Rhys Ifans, another effortlessly cool bloke, in a pub and he agreed that he was in my shadow when in each other's company. The fact he had the self-confidence and awareness to admit this only adds to his cool. If I met someone cooler than me I'd confess to it in a shot. It's never happened but if it did. So what I am saying is: please don't be gulled by the fashion industry. You are either cool or you're not and all the money in the world won't change that.

I was contemplating the correct way to act when someone shows you their new baby and it's not a looker. Now it doesn't actually matter to me what a baby or anyone else *looks* like, everyone just looks like they look, but one cannot help notice in extreme cases that some new-borns lack in the classical aesthetic appearance area. They may well develop, like the duckling of folklore, into a beauty when they mature of course but don't say that! So what do you say – 'Oh yes'. Or 'I see ... yes.'? I don't know. It's like you go to see a friend in a play and they are rubbish. What do you say in the bar afterwards? 'Interesting' or 'it was brave.' You can't just say 'That was shit and you were shit in it.' Though I have had it said to me on several occasions. You can say it to a friend who knows the score of course, but the baby is more difficult. Anyway I have come up with 3 things NOT to say.

'Christ he/she's ugly!'

'Is it a proper baby?'

'Is that its real head?'

Avoid these things. Pretend the baby is within acceptable parameters. It may be a little white lie but it's kinder. I'm sure the parents are fully aware that they have produced a genetic anomaly. You don't need to underline it. I hope this advice helps when you are next placed in this insidious situation. And also be vigilant in not betraying your true reaction by unguarded physical expression, recoiling for example, or covering your mouth. New parents can be very sensitive. Take care.

In a conversation today someone referred to 'the lesbian and gay community'. It is a common enough phrase, one hears it regularly, but it set me pondering on the usage of the word 'community' in such a context. Surely lesbian and gay people are classic examples of Diaspora in that they are spread worldwide. A community comes from commune, a coming together of people in a specific space, hence a village community or a school community or a church community. If diaspora were considered communities it would spawn endless examples e.g. the thick community, the paranoid community, the semi-literate community, the non-swimming community, endless as I say. I myself would belong to both the depressed and the apple crumble and custard eating communities to name but three ... the innumerate community! Am I failing to see something here? Is this a new addition to the definition of 'community' that I haven't heard about?

I hate sunny weather. I love the rain. I love cold sparkling black winter nights. I love kissing girls in the rain, walking hand-in-hand through storms, lying in the semi-light of a bedroom together listening to the symphony of precipitation playing out on the roof and windowpanes. Women look lovely in sunshine and in rain of course. All wrapped up in hoods and shiny overcoats or laughing beneath blue skies, their legs, the backs of their holy necks, their ... don't get me started. Yes of course women control the weather, it is their servant, but men!! My god is there any more repulsive sight on earth than a man strutting down the road with his shirt off like a genetically modified rooster? Their grotesque chests and stomachs glistening like the skin of lizards for all to see. It is also undeniably true that these pathetic popinjays are exposing their reptilian torsos not to attract women; I cannot believe that any woman, no matter how sexually desperate, could ever be attracted by such displays, but to impress and attract other men. It is quite simply a fact. Any man who walks about in public with his shirt off is gay. That's fine, no problem, but the annoying thing is that the vast, overwhelming majority of these effete prancers don't think they are. They actually believe themselves to be heterosexual! Oh god, the way they glance sideways at their own puppet-like reflections in passing shop windows, the way they remove their Ray Bans for a moment and smile. An army of Tom Cruise clones infecting our city centres, seaside towns like pink rabbits. How anyone could fancy them is beyond me; even their gay brethren. I mean gay men have dignity and taste. They don't just drop everything and drool at the sight of a chicken-like torso. These guys have got it wrong and their wrongness is upsetting the enjoyment of shoppers and holiday makers alike. No, give me the thick white clouds of winter.

I must point something out here. When I say I can't imagine any woman fancying these shirtless creatures, in fact I have never been able to comprehend any woman fancying any man above me. It may sound arrogant but it's true. Not now of course. I'm an old disintegrating sack of corrupted flesh now but the younger me … I'd be a better bet than 95% of men now. Yes if I was a woman I'd rather one kiss from me than a weekend in the Paris Hilton with any other bloke. It's to do with passion you see, charm and unhidden desire. Let's face it men are not attractive creatures. I have endless respect for our lesbian sisters. I have many friends of such a persuasion and love them. I've got dozens of their videos too. No, I know that the world must be peopled and Darwin will have his way but I sometimes think that it would be better for the human race to knock all this shagging on the head and just wait for us to peter out with a bit of dignity. We could wait on beaches in autumn. We could hold hands and watch the night fall. We could kiss.

Till then, you blokes keep YOUR SHIRTS on! We don't want to look at your bodies. Act with a bit of bloody decorum. Love, Boyd.

I was walking up Albany Rd yesterday when I saw a group of people standing on the pavement. As I got closer I noticed that two of them, both male, were built like Mr Universes, bulging muscles forcing their way out of skimpy black vests. I then noticed that the group were standing outside one of these tanning studios. They were all as brown as nuts. The conversation I picked up as I passed was all to do with being brown. Now, as you know, I detest sunlight and men without their shirts on though these fellows seemed nice enough and were obviously obsessed with having big muscles etc. and there are some people who find it attractive, so good luck to them. The thing is, it got me thinking about our modern addiction to the perceived as opposed to the actual. These people wanted to be brown because they believe it signifies having been in the sun a lot, abroad probably, and that they enjoy a healthy lifestyle. But it isn't necessarily true. They probably go to a gym a lot and on from there to the tanning salon. The reality of their lives is disguised and they are happy with it that way. I began musing on this. It is very much a core part of the concept of celebrity isn't it? To be admired or thought of highly without being what you portend to being, creating a doppelganger you in fact to represent the you you are dissatisfied with in a better, more desirable light. I thought of other ways of doing this. One could learn Einstein's Theory of Relativity by heart say, and recite it to people you meet in the park or the coffee shop. This would make them think you were intelligent and well-educated. You could study film reviews and hone in on a particular genre, French Existentialism for example and talk about it at length despite having never seen such a film in your life and not even knowing what existentialism means. Dress up like an off-duty doctor! Carry a rugby ball about with you claiming you've just been for a practice session. Say that you are an actor and talk about Brecht vs Stanislavsky. Say you think both approaches can be useful and it all depends on the individual. Give examples, demonstrate, like the man on the street corner telling a crowd about a traffic accident he'd just witnessed. Tell them not to show their pretty feet! You don't need to have the faintest idea what you are talking about no more than the nut-brown body builder needs to have been out in the sunlight as often as Dracula. We can come across how we want to come across and that will make us less unhappy! Or will it? As the great Sam Goldwyn said 'What really matters in this business is sincerity. Once you can manage to fake that, you've got it made!'

#62

At the vicarage, we find the REVEREND staring open-eyed at his reflection in a large bedroom mirror. Hypnotised by his own beauty, he strips naked and, confronted by this classical vision, gasps in ecstasy. He decides to spend his life savings on commissioning a statue of himself au naturel for the church. Next day he tells MRS OWEN of his plan and visits a local sculptor's studio. He eulogises his own perfection and finds it impossible not to disrobe again. Marvelling at the classic quality of his own body, the folds of fat across his midriff, the skeletal sunk in chest, the puffed-up rubbery face, he decides there and then that he will never wear clothes again. It would be an insult to the Creator's wonderful work.

LOVE & LOSS

THE SILENCE

We lay in bed
Your back to me like a great wall
And I cry just loud enough
For you to hear,
Just physical enough
For you to feel.
You ask me what's wrong
And I tell you
I am afraid
That you don't love me anymore
And the silence grows
Into a roar.

I got divorced in 1996. It was for a second time and I was crushed. Divorce is a terrible experience even when there are no other parties involved and no hatred. It signals the end of something that was once eternal, the end of eternity in fact. It makes a person question everything about themselves, their goodness, their lovability, their gullibility, their honesty. The worst part is that when you share love with someone, you share every aspect of yourself. The tendrils of intimacy entwine you in a delicate and perfect unity and on divorce, or indeed the breakdown of any long term relationship, the walls of the Castle of Love crumble down around you. In short: you are broken. Anyway, they say you'll get over it and they are right. Life has a way of carrying you along. I am not a confident person. I don't have a great self-image. It's to do with my childhood, my upbringing in the valleys and, of course, my depression. Anyway, a few months ago I was talking to my ex-wife on the phone (we get along fine) and in conversation she told me that a great contributor to our marriage's breakdown was that I was away working, acting, for so many extended periods and she was lonely and missed me. This may sound obvious to you but believe it or not in all my anguished analysis of what happened it had never crossed my mind. A few days later I thought about it and realised that I have never believed that anyone would not be pleased, relieved even, when I was away from them. I have never believed that anyone could have valued my presence. It made me cry. How can I not believe that? I miss others, those I love, friends, but my feeling of unworthiness denies me the emotion of knowing that I am missed.

I Drifted Towards Her Like Deep and Powerful Currents

I was walking home past the church.
She was sitting on the low wall that ran along the sewer
Opposite the fruit warehouse that is now a funeral parlour.
I sat beside her and we smoked a cigarette
as the rats disappeared into the blackberry bramble.
She was slender, a mauve ghost in the cigarette smoke,
lit by the stars and the intermittent flashes from the headlamps
of passing cars.
I held her swanlike neck as we kissed.
She moved my other hand from her thigh in a parody of
innocence.
Not a parody, no, she was innocent.
We parted, she disappearing into the blackness of the park.
Me, up High Street to my house where my old man was still
awake,
sat in his chair, smoking a Woodbine, waiting for me to come
home.
I went to bed and slept.
She would have been walking alone along the unlit lanes
That took her past the Non Political Club
Then home to her cold house.

The mauve ghost and I met again that night in a dream.
Her brutish brother watching us
His stinking breath pouring out of him like dragon smoke.
She swung on a swing in the park like a child.
They said that she was common.

They said that she was dirty
But they did not see her in God's embrace.
They did not taste her lipstick or smell her perfume.
No-one could condemn that holy child
Had they been there on that hillside wild
And seen her soft against the brilliant sky.
She was crying out for love
And so was I.

#66

I got home about eight a.m., my friend Bob picked me up from the train station and drove me up to Ton. I'd been acting in a one-man play at The Bush Theatre in London and had a message that my old man was very ill. He'd been suffering from cancer of the stomach, the news was not unexpected. As we arrived I noticed some strange men hovering around outside the house, they were dressed in black, they looked like ravens. Ool, my father, had died a few hours before I'd got there. I went in and went upstairs to the small bedroom I'd shared with him till I was ten-years-old. It was a grey morning and his body looked so small, so wasted away lying there beneath the sheet and blanket on the single bed. I sat beside him on a chair and looked at his face, thin and expressionless, almost alabaster in the pale light. I held his hand. He had loved me all my life. He'd saved me after my real father died. He took me in and kept me safe. I had worshipped him as a child but we'd grown apart as I got older and pursued my own way. I hadn't been home enough. I was self-obsessed, foolish and unthinking. Why, I don't know. I should have spent more time with him when he was ill. I should have sat opposite him, one each side of the fire, and balanced our feet on each other's like we did when I was a lanky teenager. I should have let him know that I loved and admired him. He was a damned fine man: honest, decent, caring and faithful to his friends. He could keep a secret. He gave considered advice. Eventually I lay down beside him on the bed, held his fragile body in my arms and cried. Dear old man. My eyes are welling with tears writing this. The room, known intimately to me, became unreal as if a set on a stage. The Freemasons call God 'The Great Architect', but we actors call him 'The Great Set Designer'. Anywhere, any room, any corner of any field or pathway through a wood where

115

death or love takes place is transformed into a shrine by the very fact. I sat on the stairs of a house once listening to my wife packing and walking out the door and that stairway led nowhere. My sister Audrey died in Sweden when I was not there. I miss her every day. No matter how you figure it, I'll be gone too one day in the not too distant future. I hope that before then I will have expressed my love and thanks to all those who have been so kind, so dear to me in my life. They know who they are but I still need to say it, to remind them that they live in my heart. It's a rainy day. Peace brothers and sisters. This, what we see, what we hear, it's the sea.

What's on my mind? You! The very concept of other people actually existing, with other lives, other memories, other desires, loves and dreams. It is by far the strangest and most poignant of concepts. This is why falling in love is so wonderful, that you get to interact intimately with another person's tender self, the unguarded beauty. To hear of her childhood, her family life, the holidays she went on, the games she played on beaches, to kiss the same lips that lived those far away things. To taste her breath, cool and pure, from those tear-sodden lungs. And to find out about what she is now, the result of all that delicate history, to lay with her and watch her breathing in the early morning light, to watch her walking, to hear her laugh. I have loved all these things. To become a part of her life, to be allowed in to that private garden and see her as she really is, all these things are wonderful beyond hope.

PS

I am alas not perfect by any means. I think I'm hard to live with. I don't try to be but I am a tense and often foolish man. I find it hard to be myself a lot of the time and I'm emotionally frightened. I've had great love affairs but they faded with time. I still treasure them and the beautiful women involved and remain close to them but I guess the truth is that though romantic and loving, I also am an arsehole. Love is a many-headed beast. I drift like others through its complexities and do my best but that has often not been good enough. I suppose what I'm saying is that I am a human being. I do believe however that Love can neither be created or destroyed – Boyd's First Law – and the thing that was us exists forever as fresh as on that first day in the stars somewhere, waltzing in timelessness.

Listen. I don't know if it will mean anything to you but I feel I have to say it, just this once, to let you know that I love you. It has, I am sure, never crossed your mind, you are loved by so many. I can't imagine any man not wanting you. I have loved you since the moment I first saw you. You were sitting on a wall in the garden of a house at a party, you were with a long-haired bearded guy and you were both pretty drunk. You had been engaged to a friend of mine and he joined you to say hello; I stood to one side, behind him, and watched the awkward encounter. It was a black autumn night and you were lit by the dull yellow light that came from the kitchen. It was kind of unreal. I was probably pretty drunk too. Anyway I was pole-axed by your beauty. The night, the stars, the universe above faded into nothing in comparison. I didn't speak. There was nothing I could say. You were unreachable. The boyfriend and the old fiancée were talking to you but I could see that you were somewhere else way beyond where they could reach you. I felt your infinite sadness. I thought of you, and only you, for days, months, after that. The next time I saw you was in town, a bitter winter's afternoon. You were wearing a woollen hat and your face was pink with the cold. We said hello and I wanted to ask if you wanted to go for a drink but you were late meeting someone. I kissed you once. I put my hand on the curve of your hip, on your skin, it was like touching the mother of your child, and your mouth was warm and filled with sweet ambrosia. Nothing came of it. I think about you often. I think about us making love. (We are naked in a hotel room. I hold you in my arms, I smell the sweat on your thighs.) It's lust yes, but not just that. I love you. I love you with a passion and desire that never wavers. Nothing in this world, nothing in this life, can ever change that. Anyway, there you go. I've said it. To know that you are loved, to know that you are the object of an honest man's desire cannot be a bad thing and when your life comes to an end it may be a small jewel in its story. Love.

Contemplating the different qualities of so called 'reality'. Many years living with someone you love unconditionally ... one day you are confronted with it being over ... you are lost ... you move to stay with a friend, she moves to another town. You are sitting on your bed a few months later. There is a knock on the door. It's her. She has been to Paris and brought you a gift, two beautiful, flowery shirts. She knows that if you see something you really love you buy two. She is looking beautiful, ethereal even. She sits for ten minutes, you talk. These ten minutes are real. They consist of sixty second periods run together, flowers decay imperceptibly, tea is drunk, dogs and children play in fields, waves fall on beaches and the world creaks on. You are there in a room with someone you love, have loved for many years, someone you have known intimately with whom you have shared dreams and the deepest emotions with a chasm between you the size of death. You form meaningless words, you listen to your heart beating, your breath, you stare at her, past her through the window at the shapeless infinite beyond and float in the nothingness of your ghostly shared past. Now this is reality but it certainly doesn't seem anything like the realities you have experienced before this. You are aching to fall at her feet, to take her in your arms and hold her, to cry, to tell her that you are ... what? You know everything that can be said has already been said. To create an explosion of pantomime grief would frighten her, hurt her, toy with her guilt and grief. You want to be pitied? So you sit there, you play the game, you breathe in the toxic air. You watch yourself in a dream and listen to yourself speak then she is gone, back to her new life without you, back to her new world where she, being lovely, will be loved anew. You sit there. It is late afternoon on a grey winter's day. This my friends is reality?

#70

There was an article in *The Times*, I think, which said that 'seeing' a recently deceased relative, husband, wife, child etc. after they have passed on is not uncommon. In most cases these are illusions, that is, there is someone there in the street or on a passing bus who your mind convincingly mistakes for that person, but in a lesser number of cases they are actual hallucinations, that is, there is no-one there at all and the vision is totally created by the mind. This is not a sign of madness but a known symptom of grief. Even more common is hearing the departed speaking to you. This is extremely common. Throughout my childhood I 'spoke' to my father who died when I was three. I asked him questions and felt he related answers to me to those questions, not in words, but by placing them in my mind. Matter can neither be created nor destroyed. Something remains transformed into a new form. I believe this is also true of love. I think that many bereaved people who experience such phenomena worry that there is 'something wrong' with them but as the article made clear they are just reacting in a natural and understandable way. So don't worry. It's fine. We are all together in this. Love to you all.

THERE WAS ANOTHER

There was another I loved once
As I love you now.
We were perfect together
As we are now
And in summers and winters
We loved
And in light and darkness
By seas, in cities
Beneath trees
We loved.
In all these places
In every season
In heat and cold
Beneath the same sun
Though it hung in a younger sky
We loved
And that love, like this love
Will never die.

Met a girl at a John Clark's Scientific Leather Measurement course in Street in Somerset in 1970. She was blond and pretty, I was a hippy in a green afghan coat. We didn't talk much, just a chat at a social evening in a pub. When I got home she sent me a letter saying she had two tickets to see Mark Bolan at the Wintergardens in Weston where she lived and asking if I'd like to go with her. Her parents said I could stay in their house. I didn't reply. I don't know why because she was lovely and she was so brave to write the letter. I regret it to this day. I was lying in bed the other night listening to Floyd and she waltzed into my mind. I imagined that I did go to see Bolan with her and that I kissed her outside the Wintergardens. I imagined I stayed in her house that night and that we became boyfriend and girlfriend. I half dreamt that we fell in love. She came to Tonyrefail to meet my family. We walked up the Glyn Mountain on a warm summer's evening and made love in the long grass. I could taste her beautiful breath; I felt her beautiful lips against mine. We got married. I liked her family; they were younger than my parents, more modern in keeping with the times. We both carried on working in office jobs and moved to somewhere outside Bristol, equidistant between our families. After a time she got pregnant and she stopped work and I became the breadwinner. In my present life I went to Australia to live and pursued a life of drunkenness and drug-taking debauchery, but I was a good husband in this alternate reality. We grew old together, had grandchildren. She grew more beautiful. I was strangely content. I have never been content in my present life. As I lay there I began to feel a profound, almost overwhelming, nostalgia for this unlived life. I cried for its delicacy, it's unexperienced beauty. It was like it was a child that died in the womb. That lovely girl, who I never kissed, filled my heart and I became intensely aware that every moment, every thought, every decision taken changes everything. We each have thousands, millions of paths unchosen and each one represents a different possible life. Maybe in that life I wouldn't have had so much what society considers 'success' but I would have had love and I am sure that that is what true success is: to love and be loved. When I am lying on my bed in another twilight, that of my death, in that last immeasurable silence when there is no need to pretend anymore I think that I will measure out my life in individual moments of love, pinpricks of lovelight in the sky outside my window and kissing that blond-haired girl, the wife I never had, outside the Wintergardens on that night will be one of them. There are so many people I could have loved. Anyone can love anyone else. It's just those momentary choices that decide.

COLD, COLD IS THE WIND THAT BLOWS

Listen to me darling young girl with the beautiful breasts.
I am calling to you through time
From the living grave,
From the lane behind the church,
From the cold mountain in the starlight
From the garden
From the house of the mad

I remember every moment of our time together
Your gentle eyes and soft laugh
The Holy Television bathing us in its light
How you mentioned your father
How I couldn't breathe
How you opened yourself to me in innocence
Like the child you were.

We lay through the night
Till the birds began to sing
I remember how I was angered at your frailty
At your delicate chastity
The terrible way I spoke to you
Oh the unforgiveable lack of love
Oh the piercing light

And in remembering I could tear out my tongue
I could rip out my heart and my brain
I could scream my disgrace to the tingling stars
Not a day goes by when I am not ashamed
To think that such a thing is within me.

Cold, cold is the wind that blows
Black, black that never ending night

Because you were beautiful
And loving
And honourable
And I was none
I will sleep now
And send my thoughts back to their depths
Because otherwise
I would be consumed.

#74

We buried our beloved girl Lottie in the garden today. She died in my arms on Monday after a short illness. Her beautiful little body was scattered with rose petals and she was soft and fragrant in death as she had been in life. I prayed for her but realise that prayer is not necessary for such a perfect and undefiled soul. She has been our constant companion for seventeen years and I love her more than I have ever loved anyone. She often slept with her lovely head on my chest and would wake me for her breakfast by pushing it into my bearded chin and mewing insistently. One day she and I will meet again in the hereafter, both particles of undying energy in the River of Souls. It is not possible for me to express my grief. There are no words. Suffice it to say that I will think of her every day for the rest of my life and I thank the hand of fortune that she chose to share her angelic self with me. Rest in Peace my delightful, perfect girl. Your Daddy and Mummy love you. I am shedding every tear I have but it is for me I cry not you. You are in Heaven.

THE LIE

How can he look at her like that
Knowing what he knows?
Knowing he betrayed their love
When the river froze,
Knowing he had loved another
Beneath the watching moon
Up there on that hillside
And in that unlit room.

How can he kiss those trusting lips
And lay upon that bed?
Pretending that he's faithful still
When honesty is dead,
Pretending that the stars still shine
Up in the watching sky
When all there was is thrown away
Who thought such love could die?

ANTHROPOLOGY

'Is this a dagger which I see before me ... or is it but a dagger of the mind?' I gave up smoking in 1978. I was about to go on stage with The Lemmings at the Milky Way in Amsterdam when I realised I couldn't breathe. I thought if this carries on I'll die! I used to smoke twenty to thirty a day. Had done for years. I knew I had to stop. It was a piece of cake. I saw that it would only be hard if I continued to see myself as a smoker – if I romanticised smoking. If I imagined myself sat on a beautiful beach in the moonlight for example or walking along hand-in-hand with a beautiful woman or holding a press interview discussing the enormous success of my new album, I always had a fag in my hand. It was how I saw myself, cool, deep, sexy and smoking a cigarette. The way I stopped smoking was to first stop seeing myself smoking in these romanticised scenarios. I became a non-smoker in my mind and my body followed. I have never smoked another fag to this day. Forty years. The same system worked with booze. Thirty years, not a drop. We live out the dramatic contexts we create for ourselves. Society has a huge hand too, of course, advertising, the media in general imposing lifestyles on us, telling us how we should be to be cool or whatever. 'A dagger of the mind.' The rise in knife murders in Britain is a result of a generation of young people who see themselves as reflections of the American gang culture. They see themselves as being Crips or Bloods: violent, drug-addicted, promiscuous, streetwise and ultra-cool. Television and modern music have romanticised this image for decades. The pigeons have come home to roost. There are things that can be done, more police obviously, harsher sentences, social care, better, more targeted, education and psychological backup. All these things can help address the everyday violence but nothing will ever truly change until, like me, the young people involved change their self-image, the dramatic contexts in which they see themselves. This is a long term thing and can only happen if society itself changes its course away from the celebrity and greed-obsessed cult of the self to a more honest, gentler realisation that we are all one, brothers and sisters, neither better nor worse. Until we stop living a life of fear in fact. None of this will happen because we are led by people who are insulated from the consequences of their actions by wealth and privilege. It is heart breaking.

DEATH CAMP

Martha Anne loaned money to people in the war
And they paid her back with interest, the widowed and the poor.
She kept the coins they gave her in a bag tied to her wrist
And the names of those who could not pay her were written
  on a list.

Martha bought their houses cheap when they were repossessed
And rented them to the families who had been dispossessed
These houses that had once been theirs before she came along
With their men folk in the war many thought it wrong.

Martha died of cancer in nineteen-fifty-four
Alone in her unheated house behind a padlocked door
They say that she weighed just four stones; that she had lived
  on scraps.
They say that she was skin and bone there among the rats.

They found a faded photograph in a kitchen drawer
Austria where she was born in eighteen-ninety-four
Three pretty girls in ribbons, a man sat on a chair
A woman stood behind him with long cascading hair.

They found a letter scrawled in pencil in a dusty box
Saying that they were all fine and they thought of her a lot.
And another letter from the army saying they had died
In a camp in Poland in nineteen-forty-five.

Search as they did they never found the fortune she had made
She took the knowledge of its whereabouts with her to the grave
When Martha Anne was buried not many people went
There was no love for Martha Anne. Her credit had been spent.

#78

I was walking up Wellfield Road from the library and I saw a youngish bloke sat on the pavement begging. I thought 'Here's another one!' I was fed up with being harassed and made to feel guilty all the time. He was young and fit, why in God's name was he sat there begging when he could be putting the same effort into getting his life together? I determined to stride past in a huff, maybe give him a condemnatory stare. As I got closer I saw he was reading a book. He couldn't even be bothered to actually beg! I was angry. Then as I got right up close I saw that he wasn't 'reading' the book; he was colouring it in with crayons. He was concentrating intently not to let the colours spill over the defining lines. He was colouring in a cow.

The dear fellow was a child in a man's body, an innocent lost little chap, and I had condemned him from my lofty perch as some sort of disgraceful charlatan. Get up close before you judge. Our society has become cruel and pitiless under our succession of amoral and vindictive leaders. The relentless nature of their unkindness and lovelessness has permeated even the kindest of our hearts. No one is immune to their dark virus. There is a siege at the Castle of Love. We need to be constantly vigilant. X

They are here among us everywhere but they are not us, they look different, they smell different, they are alien. They plant themselves in places where we have lived happily for centuries. They don't try to integrate, they don't try to speak our language or understand our ways and what do they contribute? They don't work, they laze about in the sunshine and rain, they ignore us. They think they are better than us. They look down on us with disinterest, they stick to their own gathering together in impenetrable masses and yet ... and yet I love trees. They bring beauty. They bring a glorious diversity, innocence and grandeur to our city streets, woods, and parks. I love their individuality, their wisdom and imperturbability. Kiss a tree you'll see what I mean. Kiss one of the Seven Beauties in Roath. Kiss Rain with the glorious hanging locks.

DEPRESSION

#80

When I look at my face in a mirror, it looks like a four-pound bag of self-raising flour. No worn character, no map of a complicated journey, no lines of truth or accumulated wisdom and experience, just a two-dimensional flesh potato with indeterminate shades of sickly pink. I'm ugly as hell, that's the truth of it. Some ugly faces make up for it with ruggedness or mystique, scarred, battered, by what? What happened to hew that visage from a virgin hillside? Think Willem Dafoe, Rod Steiger, even Timothy Spall god forbid; ugly men saved by an underlying indefinable. Not me! There's nothing there behind those tiny fear-filled eyes. My nose and mouth are what you would find in the cast away bin at a sausage factory. My cheeks are puffy pasties overlain with second-hand human skin. My throat is fat, hanging like the throat of a tired toad sat on a moss covered stone by a tired stream. My body does not bear talking about. It is beyond hope. This is my future, a hopeless soul within a decrepit body. Some days I look at my reflection and see a sort of well-worn dignity. I see things I like: kindness, honesty, naughtiness and lust, but these days are becoming few and far between. I was never Brad Pitt but I was young and had the sparkle that youth brings and I was loved by women and felt at ease with myself. I am afraid. Not of anything physical but of unknown intangibles. I feel like crying and screaming out into the sky. Ah ... there! You see I am depressed! I only just realised it! Yes! So often it passes for everyday thought. It's good to know I am depressed. Love to you all.

I used to read a lot when I was younger. One book stayed with me. It was called *I Am Legend*, and it was about a man who was immune to the effects of a plague that had turned everyone else in the world into vampires. They were vampires before the plague killed them and after they died their corpses became reanimated and they would carry on as they were before death, looking for blood that is, only now they were dead so the world consisted of both living and dead vampires. The man barricaded himself into his house with food and guns and water and whiskey and the vampires, mostly dead ones, would gather on the lawn outside his house every night when the sun had gone down and throw stones at the door and the boarded up windows, calling for him to come out. Dead women would expose themselves to him and one of the dead men who'd been a neighbour in life called out his name repeatedly in a flat vampire voice. The man was losing his mind needless to say. He stayed drunk most of the time. Other things happened in the book but I can't remember them. I remember him though, the man. He reminded me of me and at the time when I was reading the book, I think I started to actually believe that I was him. I'd look out of my window at night and think I saw them, the dead, gathering outside. I'd hear them calling out to me as I closed my eyes to try to sleep. I even heard one special one repeating my name and it echoing in the darkness – 'Boyd! Boyd Clack! Come out Boyd!' It drove me mad. There were other things too. It was like I was dreaming a lot of the time. Once I heard a solitary drum being beaten in the street outside my bedroom window and was sure that it was at the head of a host of people, poor people, marching in silence but for that drumbeat to my house. I realised after a time that it was my heart beating. These are the things that shaped me. Are you the same?

I was sitting on my own in the back room of my house looking through the French windows at the garden in the moonlight. One moment I was thinking an ordinary thought and a moment later I was sitting on a faded throne in a cavern miles below the earth. There were things moving in the dim flickering light, grey things, shadows sliding from place to place, animated things, things with eyes, malevolent things, things without thought. I felt sick. The nausea intensified till it became everything. I wanted to move, to cry out, but I couldn't. The walls and the stones in the cavern began to slide in concert with the thoughtless things. They created an awful oppressive gravity that nailed me to the faded throne. I was helpless and my soul was being corrupted. There was a stone the size of a human head inside my chest and my brain stung as if it had been bitten by a venomous snake. I realised that I was in Hell and it was where I had always been. I often dream that I am in Tonyrefail: it's sort of the present but the place is greyer, almost Gothic in appearance and mood. I am walking up High Street from the square. I am going to visit my home where I was brought up but as I walk along I become aware that I am being observed by people who hate me and wish to do me ill. The walk is fraught with danger. I don't know any of them yet some are like brutish versions of people I do know. They follow me with their eyes from doorways and grey buildings. One of them goes into the Red Gate to announce my presence to others of their kind who filter out to join him. I am terrified. I don't know what I am supposed to have done for them to despise me like this. It feels as if they have been waiting there, drinking, getting drunk and stewing in this hatred, for me to turn up. I start to realise that they are not fully human. They might be witches or demon worshippers. I pretend to ignore them. I keep my eyes on the pavement a few yards in front of me as I pass St David's Church but the terror grows and takes a grip of me. I know that I am about to be attacked, overwhelmed by force of numbers and I will be taken somewhere, some designated place where unspeakable evil will be wrought on me, some dark ruined house where I will be ripped apart, tortured and devoured in a dreadful ritual. My soul is going to be sucked from my body and spat into the blackness of the surrounding woods.

The two experiences above are things I have experienced while in the grip of clinical depression. Both traumatised me such that I have never been able to speak of them to anyone. Look, I don't really know why I'm sharing this. I just feel as though I should now that I can express it. Many others never get this opportunity. They are trapped inside their hells forever. For them then. Don't shun them. Love them. They are helpless and innocent like children and animals.

THE MAN OF FLOWERS

I once sailed the blood red sea
To find the crocus of malignancy
But when I found land
All that was there
Was the white rose of despair

The shifting of tectonic plates
Had created islands in the lakes
Islands that just grew and grew
Day by day
Though no-one knew.

The islands formed a continent
Which no-one loved
Where no-one went
A broken place of withered trees
Newly born but killing me.

What happened to the huge flocks of birds that used to darken our autumn skies years ago? All those tiny souls soaring as one, those little hearts beating as one. They'd swoop and swirl into beautiful shapes, funnels of wingbeat, ever-changing shorelines and ghosts and angels. Today's skies are darkened with disillusionment and fear I'm afraid, no little lives going about their business, just sadness made abstract. I was standing in a garden late at night in London, my garden small but sweet, when I saw a pale lilacness escape from the slightly open upstairs window of the house next door and soar of into the black sky and I realised that it was the ghost of Love. The couple there had split up and the girl stayed there alone. Poor lost soul, crying at her dressing table, looking at her face in the mirror through dark eyes. I could have died there. I knew a woman who drowned in a huge vat of vodka and pineapple and a man I worked with who threw himself off the roof of the building he lived in after Sophie left him for a poet. We are the shotgun children. Brian was buried in a tiny churchyard down a winding country lane near the sea. There was a sunshower. My hands are old, my fingers thin, like talons. Where are the snows of yesteryear? Why this waiting? Waiting for what? Are we waiting for what might have been to become what is? I think we are. I think we cling on waiting for magic to happen, for mistakes to be righted in retrospect – for the story to be rewritten. We are dreamers then. Last moments, the silver paper burns, so that was it ...

FLEETWOOD LANE

Seventh day of February, 1789

Walking on Fleetwood Lane this morning, the sun low ahead dazzling mine eyes, when all the host of people walking in the opposite direction seeking shops of various kinds became as shadows or ghosts, each one drifting by seeming to greet me in a pleasant manner and I was distracted from reality as if a man in a dream or indeed walking to heaven. This following the recent showering of bright sparks in mine eyes and mind and the flickering visions of still repose that laid me low in spirit for many days has convinced me that ought is real or as it seems but all is as vapour and this world but a chimera. I saw also a host of angels sat on the branches of several trees in the great park and wondered at their business.

The great Hamlet soliloquy 'To be or not to be …' basically says that the reason people don't kill themselves when faced with the untold horrors, unfairness and hopelessness of life is that they fear what comes after death could be even worse. It's a persuasive and beautifully expressed philosophical idea and easy to agree with. I am sure it is true for many but on contemplation I realise that it is not true for me. I don't fear death or what comes after it. In fact I don't care what comes after death. If there is something, an Elysian field, a pit of writhing demons or, as I suspect, the everlasting nothingness that the Kabala tells us we emanate from then so be it. I won't be the first and I won't be the last. No, it doesn't trouble me. The reason I don't kill myself is that by staying alive till death reaches out for me the possibility of something wonderful happening remains. It may not, it probably won't but it may! Wonderful things have happened to me in the past even when in the pit of my despair. I have fallen in love, I've had divine visions. I have created works of beauty that lifted me up with the angels. Life doesn't guarantee anything like that happening but it is a prerequisite. It's the ticket to the lottery and why rip up that ticket? I realise that my apparent positivity here may come as a shock to many of my FB friends who are familiar with my morose and moribund nature but there you go. Maybe if you feel like throwing yourself off a car park roof one day you'll think of this and refrain. Yours in unexpected lightness of being Boyd XXX

GOD OF NOTHING

#87

I don't believe in God, I don't believe in magic. What I do believe is that there is a collective unconscious – a River of Souls – through which all things flow, not just people but all things that have ever lived. I align myself to this. I would have no part of any other afterlife or eternity. I believe that Life is a going out and collecting from this form of existence so as to take the treasures of this experience back to the River. Another analogy could be seen in the action of bees, leaving the hive to collect pollen then taking it back to the hive where it is made into honey. This is what all living things are doing and because we are so many we, between us, take back an almost infinite variation in types of pollens so that the hive/river increases not only in volume but in intensity and beauty and, ultimately, simplicity too. I think that everything is ultimately one thing and that thing is love.

#88

I have nothing to say. In fact it's less than that, my mind is like a desert at night. There is no hint of thought, nothing stirring in the empty expanse. Is this what the mystics seek, this passive acceptance of nothingness? Meditation is apparently defined as absence of thought; have I reached Nirvana? I see wisps of cotton like movement on the crests of distant hills, the pale blue of blackness lit by unseen stars. There is no time where I am. I am still, frozen in a moment of firelit perfection, like the wise men in Dadd's long-lost painting. This is one of the few things I like about myself: that I can drift into unlife. Goethe said 'Anything that actually happens is of no possible importance', or words to that effect, and I can see his point. Blake spoke of infinity in a flower. What takes place in our human existence is ephemeral. We are therefore we think. I have nothing to say.

GOD OF NOTHING

Walking in the country
My foot fell through the earth
Past the roots of trees
And rocks
Into a cavern where no sun had ever shone
And there in that primitive place
I saw a throne and an ancient god
Carved from living mud sat unmoving
Beneath a crown of dazzling grey
Dead and hate filled
Worshipped by scuttling things
And shadows
Embittered by centuries
Of captivity
And he stared at me
As if I were the true god that put him there
But though I was alone
In that place of dust
I felt no fear.
'Your time has come.' he said
And leant his face close to me.
His teeth were made of jagged blood.
'My time has come' I replied
'And it is mine not thine.'
And I smiled with love
And sang a song to the
Daylight and the birds above.

You will be aware of my belief that what we personify as 'God' is in fact everything. By 'everything' I mean everything in every form that exists in the infinite, or not, expanse of physical being. This explains omnipresence of course and ultimate responsibility, as Voltaire put it 'What is the point of crying over spilt milk when it took all of the powers of the universe to spill it?' My worship of nature and our fellow creatures has made me refer to myself as a Pantheist before now but in contemplating my 'everything' belief it dawns on me that the prefix 'Pan' does not refer to nature as such but to 'all' or 'everything'. In my mind this confirms that a Pantheist is indeed an accurate description of my belief system. Pan: 'All', Theist: 'Believer in'. though I have been reliably informed by a theologian friend that the word that most accurately embodies my belief structure is 'Panentheist', a subtle but distinct extension of Pantheism to include the all beyond the all of just nature. Over the last few days I have extrapolated a further detail of this belief. In contemplating 'Good and Evil' I now realise that these things do not exist in a macrocosmic sense. There is no great source of evil; no devil. Evil is simply a mutation of human genealogy. This seems so obvious to me now but I have been blind to its truth all my life. I have fallen for the 'we are playthings of dark, mystical, universal powers and energies' excuse (more or less) unquestioningly. There is no objective evil. We humans with our expanded brains and our inescapable impulse (or curse some may call it) to philosophise and create frameworks have evolved the excuse of evil to explain the dark side of our own nature, the evolved nature of our species that is. We have objectified it. No devil my friends, and since everything everywhere other than us is perfect, no 'good' either. There is no need for a separate idea of goodness in an innocent universe. Let's stop talking of evil as an intangible malign force and accept that it is our own creation made to rationalise our own corrupted nature.

#91

When a tsunami flood hit the south coast of England and Wales in the 17th century people thought it was a punishment by God for their ungodly ways. The Great Plague was thought of as the same. How weird isn't it, that people didn't only 'think' this, they knew it to be true because there was no other explanation? Today we have explanations for things but people choose not to believe them. There are many people of a so-called religious bent who believe that AIDS is a divine punishment for the 'sins' of homosexuals. The fact that it kills non-homosexuals as well is dismissed. Maybe God missed with a lightning bolt. These people are collateral damage. What of the future, if there is one? Maybe five hundred years from now there will be a mammoth earthquake destroying whole countries and the survivors will mutter, 'There go the pointy-headed ones entertaining themselves again' or, 'Well that's the bouncing diamonds hitting the fence!' It's an argument in favour of blind belief in a way I suppose. You have to believe things are the result of something or the universe has no order. I don't think that the necessity for blind belief should be an excuse to deny proven truth though. That is where I differ from the brutalists; the Dark Ages weren't called that for nothing, The Enlightenment ditto. I sometimes feel that we are entering into a new Dark Age. A time when we blind ourselves and each other with pointed sticks that have been hardened in the embers of fire. The question is of course, why? Why should we choose ignorance and stupidity over knowledge and intelligent thought? The answer lies in our inherent fear. It is what defines modern man/woman. We fear therefore we are. It is cultivated and nurtured by the power hungry hate-mongers, those who pull the strings in a practical sense, because it benefits them. Look at America. Has a country with so little to fear ever been so engulfed in it? Enemies both physical and esoteric haunt its culture and politics like mutated vermin. Americans are afraid of everything. They are afraid of not being afraid. 'The only thing we have to fear is fear itself' was not so much a statement of warning as a statement of prophetic advice. 'Therefore let's fear that.' could have been easily added. Yes, we fear each other, we fear the unknown, we fear ourselves, we fear the known, we fear our children, we fear peace, we fear love. We have come nowhere since the Dark Ages. We have rejected the only true god, the god of the underdog. It is the Twilight of the Dogs.

A thought entered my head. It was one of those incredible thoughts that seem to come from a magical place. You know how sometimes, once or twice in a lifetime maybe, you see things with amazing clarity as if you've been given access to a fundamental and wonderful truth and everything falls into place, a glimpse into infinity maybe? Well it was one of those. Anyway what came into my mind was how beautiful life is. I'm talking about an ordinary life containing the whips and scorns of time, happiness and sadness, love and hate and all the things in between. Being a depressive by nature, and having a melancholy temperament, I am usually somewhere between blue and broken but even I, with my life and my mind, can still see the beauty of life, the planet itself, nature, the universe above, the beautiful crashing seas and oceans, the infinite delight of our fellow living creatures and their delicate unsullied souls, the love of a woman, the kindness of strangers, the exhilarating dance through reality. In fact the only negatives in life are those created by my species. Everything else is perfect. So, as I say, I am aware of this but my earlier revelation was this – What if non-life, be it before birth or after death, is even more wonderful? What if it has other beauties beyond the imaginations of the living? What if it is so wonderful, so beyond what we can conceive of, that the wonders of life pale into insignificance in comparison? I am not talking about a Heaven; I am talking about a state of dynamic grace. And I wondered why is it that we are so detached from non-ego-driven thought that we don't actively consider this possibility? Man created God and therefore it is logical that the god he created raises him and her above other living things but it is not true that we are above any other form of life or non-life come to that. Life is a thing that happens between two points. Beyond that who knows what glories await?

THE LEAGUE OF
MIDDLE AGED
DESTROYED MEN

I belong to a 'secret' society. Well, we are secret not because our existence is unknown but because the fact that we are organised isn't. You will all be aware of us, we are everywhere: we are 'The League of Middle Aged Destroyed Men' or MAD Men for short. I am the chairman. The necessary entrance qualifications are simple: you need to be between the ages of forty-three and sixty-nine; live on your own in a grey charmless flat or bedsit; have been through at least two acrimonious and life shattering divorces or broken longish term relationships (or never been in any relationship – a gold star!); do your own shopping in Tescos.

A Tesco bag is a necessary accoutrement for members; lately the added pathos of the sturdier reusable bag has entered to the sad equation. You have to eat microwaveable ready meals, takeaways or junk food almost exclusively. Your clothing must be old and battered, ill-fitting jackets, scuffed leather shoes, checked shirts and second hand grey trousers or faded Levis (another gold star!). MAD Men are not attractive creatures and, with the exception of the few self-deluded ones who 'go to' the gym once a week, know it. Children one never sees are common. The ex-wife who turned them against you is a pantomime demon that haunts the fragile psyche like a succubus. We have no discernible talent except on occasion the ability to play blues harmonica. Music wise its prog rock. Yes is our house band. We are incredibly unhappy. Our lives are parodies of what we dreamt they would be when we were young enough to dream. We are plagued by bills we cannot pay. We all suffer from a permutation of the following ailments: diabetes, hiatus hernia, clinical depression, haemorrhoids, frequency of urination, hypochondria, fungal toenail conditions, impotence, dental problems and age-related deafness. We watch TV a lot, mostly documentaries and films on DVD. We have given up. There is no hope for us. We spend days walking up and down suburban and city streets hoping that we'll meet someone or something will happen. A friendly face is always a similar face; we don't integrate with the living. They fear us. We are what they dread becoming. Many of us are borderline alcoholics. We drink to feel better about ourselves, to loosen our tongues and minds so that we can express our pain in an acceptably humorous way to others of our ilk but we usually end up back at their place crying. We can occasionally be violent when drunk and have had to seek professional help at one point. Dope smoking is not uncommon. We live in a fantasy past where we were in the race, where we were sparkling and talented, where we had sex with non-professional women without paying cash. Our children pity us. We assemble regularly in places created for us over time. Nero's on Albany Road is one such place, The Old Arcade in town, another. We are drawn to such places instinctively like wildebeests to a waterhole. There are some females, broken, crushed and spat out by life, who hang about on the periphery of such gathering places. They are overweight (as are we) unattractive (ditto) and often have quite severe mental health issues. These women actually want to have sex with some of us – usually the ones who have created an illusion of character and whose looks still exist if only in pathetic parody. These women no doubt have an organisation of their own – The League of Unloved Women. If you see someone you suspect may be a member you must offer him our 'secret' handshake. This consists of contorting your wrists until they almost break. We have a tie: dark blue with an image of a skeletal leaf-stripped tree on the crest of a moonlit pathway vanishing over a distant hill with a gaunt man beneath it half-turned to face the observer.

Our Motto is 'I Tried and I Failed'. As I said we are everywhere. We are many as grains of sand on a beach. If you could harness our collective energy, it would not be enough to light a bicycle lamp. Anyway, you know who you are. If you want to apply for membership please go to Facebook group 'THE LEAGUE OF MIDDLE AGED DESTROYED MEN'. If you wish to contribute to our news sheet – 'Nothing Happens in My Life' or just express your pain please feel free. Not that anyone will give a shit but ... Hey, right. Yours in Brotherhood, Boyd

PS

Oh yes it is possible to be a MAD Man if you are in a relationship or married even provided that your partner/wife hates you and spends every waking moment belittling and trying to demean you in both your own and everyone else's eyes. Gay men can't join because they can at least still go cottaging and have sex. There's a society for them too: Gay Men Clinging On.

I am not a vibrant person. It's difficult because I used to have a sparkling energy that drove me on. I was the instigator of things artistic and a well of energy from which inspiration could be drawn. I never wanted to lead others but I really wanted to walk side-by-side with them. I need help now. I need to garner energy from other people's involvement. I really want to act more. I cannot understand how these TV plays and series can go ahead without me in them. What's the matter with these people? Don't they see that I am me? Boyd Clack! I find it ridiculous that these robotic beings are not hammering down my door, crawling all over me, inviting me to lunch in fancy Soho restaurants, offering me women and cocaine, getting me to meet young whippersnapper directors and their elderly millionaire boyfriend producers. Oh yes. Penne Arrabiata with a side dish of spinach will be the order of the day. A fickle old world I work in. Everybody loves you when times are good, when your name is on the breeze but it takes no time at all for the phone to stop ringing when success falters. The people who invited you to their parties pass you by in corridors without a glance, leaving you with a broken semi-smile of greeting frozen on your Pagliacci-like face. The stars are leaden in my sky. How the fallen are mighty.

PS
If you are a TV or film casting agent, producer or director give me some work for Christ's sake. It'll be too late when I'm dead ... except for small parts in *Pobol Y Cwm*. Lovekins Boyd 'Love in the Rain' Clack XX

I was a pretty gloomy young guy as a schoolboy. I didn't see brightness and joy all round. It was to do with my father's early death and my family being split up I've no doubt. When I was old enough to be aware of the greater world I began to despair and often found myself crying on the armchair sat by the fire. World starvation, Biafra, civil rights brutality, everyday unkindness, the type that seemed to slide off other peoples' backs cut me like a knife. Anyway, I stumbled on. When I was nineteen I started to work in the Parc Mental Asylum near Bridgend. I lived in, on one of the wards. It was an old Victorian institution, dark, oppressive, gothic, and the mood was one of mild to severe horror. While there I began to feel an often intense empathy with the patients. Schizophrenia is the most terrible of all illnesses. There were ordinary people, men and women, Welsh people like me with the same background, the same upbringing, who had somehow succumbed to the fantastical destruction of their own minds, the loss of control of their lives to a degree where they were essentially confined to a living hell. I could see no reason why it couldn't happen to me. I began to envisage a future spent in such a place, a small room in a back ward watching the seasons pass and the years go by until old age and death. I had to get out and I did but I went on to work in St Saviours Hospital in Jersey and Gladesville in Sydney till I finally turned my back on the profession all together when I was 22. The thing is that this work, mixing with these unfortunate people, sort of broke my heart. It wasn't just pity (though god knows I felt that) but it was an existential fatalism that laid me low. Where was God? Why should the innocent suffer so while the evil thrived all round? What was life? These unanswerable questions nurtured a deep fear and horrible despair in me. Another thing it did, together with my initial childhood pain, was make me identify with the weak and helpless. I began to see a poetic, almost holy, quality in the world of those who sunk beneath the waves. I began to see romance and beauty of a depth that the golden ones for whom life was easy could never even imagine. I rejected the company of the strong. I sought out the broken. I wandered in the twilight. Though I am not so tethered now I still feel drawn to those who, like me, are somewhat disconnected from the source. Leonard Cohen's novel *Beautiful Losers* touched me greatly. This was what my world was – that inhabited by beautiful losers. It is so to this day. I have had some success and there are those who would consider me a winner in many ways but I am not 'of' them. I chanced upon a bit of success. 'They' know I am not like them and have never felt comfortable in my company. I repel them in fact and they have never done me any favours. So be it. I cannot change. I don't want what they want; I don't see the world as they see it: I'm not happy but there again who is? There is a darkness that will never go away.

\#96

Someone told me recently that I should 'exercise my demons'! What sort of advice is that!? I am plagued by them all day and night, in sunshine and in shadow. If I wake in the dead of night they are there, lizard-skinned and flickering-tongued, laughing at me, taunting me, belittling me in the moonlit gloom of my bedroom. Yet I am told to *exercise* them! The only good thing about them is how unfit they are! Some of them can't even stand upright. They just recline on the floor or slither about like serpents. They are physically shot. I could outrun them at a pinch and I'm no Usain Bolt. So NO I am not going to exercise them. If any of them choose to attend a gym of their own accord then so be it but I'm not making a rod for my own tormented back. I may be plagued by demons but I'm not stupid!

I had a phone call from the Vatican today. They asked me if I would agree to be the next pope! I was quite surprised. I explained that I am not a Catholic and believe all religious organisations to be the devil's hands and ears on earth. I don't speak Latin either but Cardinal Diablo said it didn't matter. All they want is an oldish beaten-down-looking bloke with a benevolent smile superimposed on an obviously melancholic interior. An ex-alcoholic would be ideal. He pointed out that if I took the job I would get to be carried around in a chair. I am tempted. What do you think? The minuses would be that I would be the figurehead of an organisation that has historically protected, even promoted known paedophiles, the spokesman responsible for marginalising and degrading millions of homosexuals and women, the head of an organisation that walked hand in hand with fascism in the thirties, forties and fifties closing its eyes to the holocaust and facilitating the escape from justice of legions of mass murderers, insane doctors and sadistic torturers to Catholic havens in South America and I'd be helping spread AIDS and other sexually communicable diseases, not to mention encouraging overpopulation in the poorest continents on earth where millions already die of hunger and disease every year, by proscribing contraception. On the plus side though I would get to be carried around in a chair. It's a toughie. Despite its drawbacks, there are attractions. Think of all the money and political influence I'd have. Think of the opulent palaces I'd live in. I'd eat off the finest eighteenth century china, I'd walk on ancient carpets from the orient, I'd have beautiful gardens to walk in, eat the finest food, and drink the finest wines. Yes ... hmmm ... I think I'll do it! Pope Boyd the First! Would you worship at my feet? Martin Luther (no, not the bald guy from

Superman comics) referred to the then pope as 'that glittering worm in excrement'. He had a way with words. I will do it!!! Do you think I should?

Feeling mad is incredibly intense. It is grotesque, nightmarish and terrifying ... but also incredibly intense. I have heard soldiers say that a minute in a battle is like a year of everyday life due to the intensity, the focus, the realisation that it is for real. People are actually trying to kill you. You are trying to kill them. Well madness is something like that. Your mind is trying to kill you. It is like a huge Anaconda trying to crush you. Sometimes when you feel good (not mad that is) it is as if your thoughts have lost their dramatic weight, that they are unimportant, bland. Your emotions and feelings drift by without beauty or despair. You are being blown along uneventfully in an autumn breeze. I have been feeling like this for a while now. Having been under the cosh for six or seven months prior to this I am not complaining. I find however that I have nothing to say at the moment. The adventurer has come home after years at sea fighting monsters and is resting in his cottage on the cliff top. I see the light from the lighthouse revolving each night, its beam reaching out into the unseen blackness of the sea and my mind is empty. This may not make sense. It may be that I am trying to express something that cannot be expressed. It may be that I don't know what I am saying. The room is white, it is clean and neat. Love to you all.

Got hit on the head by a falling branch during a storm a few years back. I was knocked unconscious; in fact it was touch and go for a while. I 'woke' in a dark forest of gnarled trees and began stumbling through the undergrowth not knowing where I was or where I was going as if in a dream. My legs and arms were torn at by thorns and the jagged edges of unseen rocks. A nameless fear drove me on. Eventually I came to a clearing, a small canyon, ancient with the ruins of stone buildings that had been hewn from the rock on either side forming a pathway towards a statue of a huge demonic head. As I approached it I passed men and women naked and bloody hanging from hooks embedded deep in the rock. They were being prodded with spears and forks by monstrous imp-like beings. I saw people having their throats cut and their anuses penetrated with red hot pokers by cowled priests. There were men and women being turned on spits above open fires. Eyes were being burned out with smouldering sticks, tongues torn out with tongs. People were being drowned in vats of human excrement. The stench became unbearable. I stopped in front of the head. It spoke 'You come here to my kingdom, to my home, to be judged on your pathetic life in the world of sunlight and soft summer breezes.' I told him that I was unaware of this. I said the last thing I recalled was walking through the park with my dog Tina. 'Pathetic, weak fool! None of that matters any more. You are mine now. You will spend your eternity in a pit of unimaginable pain. Your soul will burn to the age-old music of human suffering. Many have come before you, each with a tale to tell. They squirm and dissemble, they beg, they implore but nothing will save them. Nothing will save you, Boyd Clack! Oh yes I know who you are! I have watched you since the dawn of time and now, now at last you are mine!!' Then he laughed. I told him I was a professional actor and he let me go.

COEDELY TWILIGHT

Was that me walking up Pant Y Brad,
Flicking the hedges with my broken stick,
Watching the birds take wing?
My old man pointed out a towering tree.
He told me it was where a great prince had hidden.
I heard a Starling sing.

We walked into the falling night,
The tiny lights of the village at our feet
Milky stars in the sky.
Coedely Colliery like a child's toy
All black iron and smoke
Nestled like a glade of bluebells in the twilight.

My old man walked slow and steady.
He enjoyed the fading of the day.
He breathed deep of the lavender scented air.
We heard the church bells ring.